GARDENING TIPS

from

Dermot O'Neill and Friends

TOWN
HOUSE
DUBLIN

First published in 2002 by
TownHouse & CountryHouse Ltd
Trinity House
Charleston Road
Ranelagh
Dublin 6
Ireland

1 2 3 4 5 6 7 8 9 10

A CIP catalogue record for this book is available from
the British Library.

ISBN: 1-86059-166-3

Cover and text design by Anú Design, Tara
Typeset by Keystrokes Ltd, Dublin
Printed by WS Bookwell, Finland

Contents

*I dedicate this book to the memory of
my late grandmother Hanora Hall.
And to my parents, whose constant encouragement
can always be counted on.*

Acknowledgements

A book like this cannot be written without the help of a great many people. First and foremost, I would like to thank all of my gardening friends who have contributed their tips and gardening wisdom to this book.

I would like to acknowledge Carmel Duignan's support and to thank her for her valuable advice and for the time she spent helping me on this project.

I would also like to acknowledge the support given from Stephen Smith.

A special thanks to all the staff at TownHouse Publishers for their diligence and patience. Thanks to Siobhan O'Brien for her help with the manuscript and also a big thank you to Ciara Bolard whose help with the initial preparation was invaluable. And for words of encouragement and for good advice, thanks also to May Kealy, Brian O'Donnell, Bill O'Sullivan and Helen Dillon.

Introduction

My grandmother and her garden greatly influenced me and I can remember, as a young boy, watching her tending all kinds of wonderful plants. I believe that I absorbed a lot of what was going on around me at the time without quite fully understanding it, and I think that my fascination with gardening can be traced back to those days watching my grandmother at work. I consider myself lucky, as gardening has always been such a passion for me that it has made creating gardens and growing plants easy. Somehow, subconsciously, my grandmother's gardening wisdom has been passed on to me.

A great many of my gardening friends also find their gardening interest rooted in early memories and this leads me to believe that truly passionate gardeners are influenced, not only by teaching, word of mouth and the books they read, but also by early observation.

A lot of my gardening has been done in restricted spaces – and often in other people's gardens – but for years I have longed to have a space large enough to realise my gardening dreams, a place where I could design and create my own garden. This dream became a reality recently when I purchased a neglected walled garden in the foothills of the Slieve Bloom Mountains – the Clondeglass Walled Garden. Like an artist with a blank canvas, I am now able to put into practice all the gardening ideas and techniques I have developed over time.

I discovered early on in my career that I enjoyed teaching and sharing information and, the longer I garden, the more I realise that there is always something new to unearth about the subject. No matter how long you have been a gardener, you never stop learning. To pass on the secret of growing a special plant or to teach someone a simple technique gives me as much pleasure as the growing of plants.

The wonder of growing vegetables has never left me. Admittedly, planting a bulb and, several months later, enjoying its flowers has its own rewards, but to raise something from seed and bring it to full fruition – where it ends up on a plate – is an achievement that should never be taken for granted. Gardening enables us to use all of our senses.

I have spent the past 25 years enjoying gardening and making it my life's work. Over those years, I have been fortunate to make many gardening friends all over the country with whom I have shared information and discussed topics ranging from the effects of weather to the latest 'must have' fashionable plant. But one of the most valuable things those friends have shared with me has been their own gardening wisdom – wisdom that has been honed by many years of hands-on experience in their own gardens. I have gained immeasurably from their personal insights into gardening techniques and practices.

Like cuttings taken from a plant, these gardeners shared their tips with a free-spirited generosity that can be found in gardening communities throughout the country. Their gardening tips, gathered together in this book, are a resource to be treasured.

All the gardeners who have contributed to these pages have one thing in common: the garden is their own special space, a place where they have the opportunity to create something for themselves, a haven of tranquillity and peace which soothes the soul and provides relief from the pressures of busy modern lives.

The tips in this book offer common-sense solutions and sound practical advice. The gardeners assembled here know that the secret to creating and maintaining a productive and beautiful garden is simple: it needs sustained regular care. Following their advice will help you to minimise the effort and time you spend working in your garden so that you will have more time for enjoyment and relaxation. In the process, your garden will become a haven.

Dermot O'Neill
August 2002

Dermot O'Neill

Clondeglass Walled Garden, County Laois

All gardeners enjoy receiving and giving gardening tips and, in the course of my work, I am constantly being asked to share my own personal tips. These tips have come from many years of gardening experience. The gathering of this experience has been a journey that has become an adventure: the adventure of creating my own garden paradise.

As a child, I can remember being taken by my grandmother to visit an old walled garden. On our arrival, I can recall the heavy, solid door to the garden, that gave an incomparable feeling of privacy and aroused my curiosity as to what lay beyond. Inside lay a garden paradise, a secret world full of beauty, an Eden separated from the rest of the world. This place stays vividly in my memory to this day.

Many years later, this memory was to help me fulfil a dream – a dream of someday owning a walled garden where I could indulge my love of plants. In recent years, I purchased Clondeglass Walled Garden, which nestles in the foothills of the Slieve Bloom Mountains in County Laois, and started the process of achieving this ambition. The garden had long been abandoned and showed very little trace of its former glory, so I immediately set about bringing it back to its original productiveness.

Clondeglass Walled Garden is over an acre of land enclosed by high sandstone walls. As is traditional with these old gardens, the site slopes gently to the south, taking full advantage of the sun's warmth. Outside the walls on the north side is a mature deciduous wood of oak and beech, planted to protect the garden from the north wind. Within the walls, the soil has been cultivated for generations. It is dark and rich and easy to work.

In my garden, I practise traditional gardening methods that I have learned over the last 25 years and, along with these, I am now able to use modern-day interpretations of old ideas. My plan is to create an extraordinary outdoor space within four walls, integrating structural design, carefully balanced with colours, textures and patterns.

Much of my inspiration has come from visiting some of the world's most celebrated gardens, where I have seen both historical and modern designs. I have drawn on these for the creation of the garden at Clondeglass.

In making this garden, I am realising a childhood dream and I hope that I never lose that sense of wonderment and magic as I step through the door into my own walled garden paradise.

Dermot's tips

1 **Potting table**

Create your own potting table by recycling an old ironing board. It will be height-adjustable and will need very little storage space.

2 **Repotting**

If roots start to appear through the drainage holes at the base of a pot, it is a good indication that the plant needs repotting into a larger container. This is best done early in the year.

3 **Creating drainage**

- Drainage holes – Check that the drainage holes in your container have been punched out properly. If not, use a drill to do this yourself.
- Drainage layer – Try using a layer or two of teabags instead of traditional crocks. Teabags are readily available and easy to recycle.
- Brick feet – Prevent drainage holes from becoming blocked with garden debris by standing your container on bricks or pot-feet.

4 **Repotting a plant**

When repotting a plant, push the old, smaller pot into the compost in the new pot. This will make a hole into which the plant's existing rootball will fit perfectly. Settle the new plant in and water well.

5 **New plants**

Pot up cuttings from tender perennials in late summer to ensure that you have plenty of plants for use the following year.

6 Taking cuttings

When taking cuttings, half-fill your pot with peat moss then fill to the top with a layer of horticultural sand. Push your cuttings in through the sand so that the base of the stem just touches the layer of peat. Cover with a clear plastic bag and you will have new plants in no time.

7 Preventing loss of moisture

Soft, young shoots lose moisture rapidly. Place cuttings in a plastic bag until you are ready to prepare them.

8 Feeding

When feeding summer-flowering annual plants, be careful not to overdo it, as too much food can encourage the growth of leaves at the expense of flowers.

9 Cut flowers

If you want to ensure cut flowers from your garden last as long as possible, water the plants the night before cutting and then cut the flowers in the early morning or late evening.

10 Frost-free greenhouse

To keep your unheated greenhouse free from frost in winter, light a few candles on a very cold night. This will do the trick.

11 Creating a focal point

Transform an expanse of green by planting a specimen tree. Choose one that will grow to a suitable size. A large tree looks confined in a small setting, and a tiny tree looks lost in a large area.

12 Makeover for a post or clothesline

If an old metal pole or clothesline is embedded in concrete and cannot be easily removed, use it as a vertical support for a climber. The denseness of the climber's growth will soon hide the post.

13 Rejuvenating a hawthorn hedge

To rejuvenate a hawthorn hedge that has become sparse and leggy at the base, bend a number of pliable stems downwards and peg them into the soil using small metal hooks. In time, these stems will take root and fill out the base of the hedge.

14 Nettle stings

Nettle stings are relieved by rubbing the sore area with dock leaves. However, you can also try garden mint, which works faster and has a suitably soothing effect.

15 Glut of tomatoes

If you have a glut of tomatoes and find that some have become overripe, you can make them firm again by placing them in a bowl of salted water for about 15–20 minutes.

16 Clematis

- Protecting the base: plant clematis several inches deeper than it is planted in its container. Use a cylinder of strong cardboard or plastic to protect the base from slugs and snails. Secure with twine.
- Extra precaution: smear a band of grease around the top of the cylinder. Slugs and snails will not be able to climb over this, so they will not reach any young stems and cause them damage.

17 Moving a heavy object

To move a heavy object from one part of your garden to another, it is a good idea to attach a rope to a child's skateboard. It can make a very good trolley for moving heavy potted plants around.

18 Garbage bag

To help keep a black plastic garbage bag open for garden rubbish, line it with a cardboard box which has had the bottom removed. This is especially useful when filling bags with garden leaves.

19 Legs of a ladder

To help prevent the legs of a ladder from sinking into the ground or damaging your lawn, place empty tins under the legs. This will help spread the weight.

20 Drainage

Retaining brick walls do not enable excess water from the soil to drain away. To prevent waterlogging, make a 'weep hole' in the lowest layer of bricks. To do this, leave a few joints empty of mortar. Ensure that weep holes are kept clear of debris.

21 Gutters or drains

When cleaning your garden in autumn, it is important not to forget to remove leaves that have become caught in gutters or drains. These can be added to your compost heap.

22 Keep drainpipes clear

Keep drainpipes clear by wedging a plastic scouring pad or ball of galvanised wire netting into the opening of the drainpipe. This will act as a filter and prevent falling leaves and other debris from clogging up the pipe or entering a water butt.

23 Using plastic bottles

Cut off the bottom of a plastic bottle and discard, remove the cap from the top part and insert this end into the compost in your growing bags. Water through the bottle, so that the water does not run straight off the top of the compost.

24 Bulbs

Squeeze a bulb gently with your thumb and forefinger. It should be firm to the touch and not feel hollow. Store bulbs in a cool, dry place if you cannot plant them straightaway.

25 Planting bulbs

Plant bulbs in groups of one variety. Try to avoid mixtures, as these will usually flower at different times, even through the dying foliage of the others.

26 Perfume

To add extra perfume to your garden late in the evening, sprinkle seeds of night-scented stock among your flowering plants.

27 Pyracantha berries

To ensure that a pyracantha is covered with berries in autumn, prune it in stages. Prune some stems in early spring, then leave these for the rest of the year. The flowers they produce will turn into berries. Cut back some of the other stems immediately after flowering.

28 French beans

When picking French beans, do so before the seeds swell and make the pods bulge.

29 Rhubarb

If your rhubarb produces a flower spike, remove it quickly or it may weaken the crown.

30 Harvesting rhubarb

When harvesting rhubarb, try not to pull more than a third of the stems. This will keep strength in the crown for next year's crop.

31 Perfect edge

To give your lawn a perfect edge, use a half-moon lawn-edging knife and slope the tool away from the edge to prevent it crumbling when it is walked on.

32 Applying seed

To help distribute grass seed evenly, use a plastic flowerpot with several holes in the base as a shaker. Once you know the area that a potful of grass seed will cover, this method will help you to sow at a consistent rate.

33 Animal urine

Dog (especially female), fox or cat urine can cause large brown patches in a lawn. Prompt action can alleviate the problem considerably. If you catch an animal in the act, wash down the area immediately with plenty of water. This will reduce the scorching effect on the grass. If you reseed an area, make sure you remove all the urine-soaked soil first, otherwise the grass seed will not germinate. Prevent animals from urinating on small areas of lawn by using plastic netting.

34 Play areas

To help protect grass under a swing or other garden play equipment, secure sturdy netting to the ground with U-shaped staples. If this does not give enough protection, reseed the area with a specially formulated mixture of tough grasses, having first incorporated ground-up tyres into the soil. Alternatively, change the surface entirely. Spread 5–7 centimetres (2–3 inches) of finely chopped bark in areas prone to damage.

35 Lawn-mower maintenance

To ensure that a lawn-mower works efficiently at the beginning of a new gardening season, have the machine professionally serviced before putting it into storage, and make sure that it is kept on a level, wooden base when it is not in use.

36 Roses

Add roughly chopped banana skins to the soil when planting roses. This improves texture and moisture retention and adds potassium.

Dead-heading roses

When dead-heading roses, cut back to just above the first leaf bearing five leaflets. This sometimes encourages an extra flower-bearing shoot.

38 Bare-root roses

When planting bare-root roses, trim back the roots by one-third. This encourages new feeding roots and helps the plant to establish and anchor itself more quickly.

39 Climbing rose

If you want to plant a climbing rose on an archway or beside a doorway, I recommend the thorn-free climber called 'Zéphirine Drouhin'.

40 Longest-possible flowering

If you are looking for a shrub that will provide the longest-possible flowering period, you will find it hard to beat *Fuchsia* 'Mrs Popple'.

41 Winter shrubs

For one of the best-perfumed winter shrubs, try the low-growing evergreen, *Sarcococca confusa*.

Hydrangeas

To turn pink hydrangeas blue, add sulphur chips to alkaline soil.

Barley straw

To stop algae from growing in water, stuff the leg of an old pair of tights with barley straw, tie both ends securely and attach a weight to the bundle before submerging it.

Vine weevils

The best way to deal with vine weevils is to soak your pots or containers with Pravado. If you are an organic gardener, nematodes can be used, but only in warm weather.

Consider your neighbours

Be a good neighbour: consider those who live around you when planting trees or large shrubs in your garden. They may affect your neighbour's view.

Shirley Beatty

Carrickmines, Dublin 18

Knockcree, where we have lived for 40 years, is a 2-acre garden on a seam of granite in the foothills of the Dublin Mountains. The rock, which I love, makes this garden, and it dictates what you can and cannot do. Because of it, the soil is acid to neutral, is very light and shallow and dries out quickly, so it is very much a spring and early-summer garden.

The garden was first laid out shortly after the house was built at the beginning of the last century. It had a nucleus of rhododendrons, azaleas, a large *Crinodendron hookerianum* and a beautiful *Drimys lanceolata*. I found the drimys lying on the ground several years ago, but, when I looked closer, I found it had left me a baby, which today is almost as big as the original. From the time Christmas is over, I look forward to the first snowdrops and with them come the hellebores, then early rhododendrons and, later on, aquilegias, which seed themselves every-where, as do ferns and geraniums. *Geranium macrorrhizum* has seeded in the crevices of the rocks in the wooded area. Nature at its best – I could never have done it!

As you pass the house and begin to climb, there is a huge outcrop of granite with a pond at the bottom where primulas grow. Behind them is an *Acer palmatum* 'Shishio Improved' and, behind that again, is a *Rhododendron griersonianum*. These all seem to blend together well.

On the other side of the path, an *Acer palmatum* 'Dissectum Atropurpureum', which I planted thirty or so years ago, hit the rock behind it and, over the years, climbed over it and now goes down to a pond. I love looking at it in the winter, when you can see its skeleton. Roses do not do well here – the soil is too light – but *Rosa xanthina* 'Canary Bird' has climbed the trellis on the house and done her own thing. It is now very large and makes a great show in the spring.

I have nearly given up on large-flowered clematis, and concentrate on the viticellas, which are so easy. I also grow *Clematis paniculata*, which climbs through a holly tree and flowers from February to April. I have the female form and am assured that the male is even better – I look forward to seeing that.

As you climb up, past a narrow herbaceous border, you come to the greenhouse and vegetable garden. To top it off, you climb some steps – granite, of course – to an area surrounded by gorse with wide-ranging views over the Dublin Mountains. Here we have planted larch, birch and similar trees and there is a seat, which is so very peaceful in fine weather. Then you descend again, through a wooded area with rhododendrons, geraniums, anemones, trilliums, etc., and so back to the house and to the lawn, which my husband, John, keeps, to set off two small herbaceous borders and a lovely early-spring wooded area. As can be gathered from all of this, gardening has been a very important part of my life and Knockcree has given my family and me great joy. I have tried to ensure that there is always something of interest, so there is always something to do and never a dull moment.

Shirley's tips

1. Feed bulbs – snowdrops, daffodils, etc. – with sulphate of potash when they have finished flowering.

2. Separate snowdrops about every 3 years. I always separate the good ones each year, if I think they need it.

3. When taking euphorbia cuttings, take the pot and compost to the euphorbia. The quicker the cuttings are put into the compost, the better.

4. Let aquilegias seed around. You never know until they flower what crosses you will get – great fun!

5. Plant for flowering in winter months, so that, when you look out of the window, you will always see something to cheer you up – for example, underplant *Prunus* x *subhirtella* 'Autumnalis' with snowdrops, hellebores and other early-flowering plants and bulbs.

6. Make sure to tidy and clean ponds before the frogs lay their spawn.

7. Cut out old and marked leaves of bergenias. It will improve their looks and stop the slugs hiding there!

8. I propagate a lot of pelargoniums, some of which are quite difficult – for example, *Pelargonium* 'Ardens'. I usually take off one of the knobs and stick it firmly into sandy, gritty compost and pray!

9 Pinch back pelargoniums. You get a much better shape and also a sturdier plant.

10 Sow the seed of *Zantedeschia* 'Green Goddess' while still green. Don't wait until they are ripe.

11 I find that the best way to propagate aeoniums is in sand.

12 Dead-head as often as possible (unless you want to harvest seed). It makes the garden look tidier and prolongs flowering.

13 Purple *Fritillaria meleagris* looks good with the red and dark forms of hellebores.

14 Put *Pulmonaria* 'Blue Ensign' beside *Omphalodes* 'Starry Eyes'. It seems to bring out the colour of 'Starry Eyes'.

15 Always make sure you cut grass verges. The best lawn never looks right unless the verges are cut. When they are, it makes the rest of the garden around the lawn area look all the better.

Jimi Blake

Airfield, Dundrum, Dublin 14

I trained in the National Botanic Gardens in Glasnevin, but my love for all things horticultural goes right back to my early teens. I came to Airfield in 1993 and was faced with the daunting task of redesigning and managing 5 acres of mostly overgrown gardens. In addition, for the first few years, I had to carry out this work alone.

I am now in my tenth year at Airfield and I have to be honest and say that the place still excites me. With the help of my team here, I have achieved a lot, but there is more to be done. My head is full of new plans and new ideas for Airfield and I hope to be able to continue to improve the garden for my own enjoyment and that of others as well.

Jimi's tips

1 Sowing seeds when ripe

Picking the right time to sow seeds depends not only on the time of year but also on the condition of the seed itself. Many seeds have to be sown fresh – so, as soon as you collect the ripe seed from the plant, sow it. For many seeds, a chilling process is required if they are to germinate at all.

2 How to get free seed

One of my main reasons for joining plant societies is for the free seed. Most plant and garden societies run seed exchanges. If you are a member of the society, you are entitled to a certain amount of free seed each year. Of course, to be fair to other collectors, it is always a good idea to send some seed that you collect yourself to the exchange – you may even get more free seed.

I ran the Irish Garden Plant Society Exchange for 2 years. It was amazing to see some of the treasures that were sent in. Some seed exchanges that I would recommend are:

- The Royal Horticultural Society, England. (Members are entitled to thirty packets of seed. It is an excellent society.)
- The Royal Horticultural Society of Ireland.
- The Alpine Garden Society, England.
- The North American Rock Garden Society.
- The Scottish Rock Garden Club.
- The New Zealand Alpine Society.
- The Hardy Plant Society.

3 Collecting seeds

Clean your seeds as soon as they are collected. If there are a lot of husks, put the seed in the palm of your hand and gently blow. No matter how small or light the seed is, the husk and chaff will always be lighter. Make sure the seed is perfectly dry before storing it. Last year I stored my vegetables in an old toolbox, which was left open throughout the winter months. I only realised recently that a family of mice had established a great hotel and restaurant in the box over the winter!

4 Compost-making – the biggest mistakes

When making compost, most people throw all kinds of kitchen waste out onto the heap, including vegetable and fruit peelings. *Stop!* This makes compost too wet, too acidic and blocks out a lot of the air. A good idea is to gather a few sacks of autumn leaves for mixing with your kitchen waste throughout the year. To this mix you can add your weeds, grass cuttings and shredded papers as before and look forward to good, healthy nutritious compost with the added bonus of knowing you did it all yourself. Having said this, I have entrusted compost-making at Airfield to one of my staff, Grainne Devaney, who seems to be much better at it than I am.

5 Watering plants in the correct way

It seems obvious to talk about watering when it comes to gardening – after all, without water we would have no garden in the first place – but it is surprising how many people just don't do it properly. They either over-compensate for hot, sunny days or they are too sparing, afraid of drowning the tender plants. The truth is that both over- and under-watering plants can be equally harmful. Of course, it all depends on the plant and the conditions it is growing in.

When watering your herbaceous borders, give them a good, decent watering. Although you may not realise it at first, you are actually doing more harm than good by only lightly watering them in hot weather. Because the water remains on the surface or slightly below it, the roots rise up in search of the moisture. The problem then is that, once they have found it, they remain close to the surface and are more vulnerable to damage. In addition, once the ground dries out again, the roots will suffer due to their proximity to the soil's surface. This is where a good mulching in the autumn really pays off.

6 Weed control

Such was the state of the South Border in Airfield that I covered it with black plastic when I first arrived and left it covered for 2 years while I got on with restoring the rest of the garden. Believe me, the plastic needs to be left for two whole seasons to effectively kill the weeds.

Please remember that, if you have to use chemicals at all, you should not wear a dust mask for protection, as these are totally ineffective. Get yourself a really decent mask for spraying. Also, don't just wear ordinary rubber gloves – wear nitrile gloves. Chemicals seep through ordinary gloves.

7 Buying decent plants and dividing them

While not every gardener may have a huge budget, when buying plants in a garden centre or nursery, it is worth spending that little bit extra on decent plants that you can take home and divide. This spring, I divided a pot of *Miscanthus sinensis* 'Gracillimus' into twenty-five plants. Twenty-five for the price of one isn't bad. The divisions I cut back and potted up in 1-litre pots and placed them under clear sheets of plastic. When growth starts again, I will remove the plastic and hopefully they should be ready to plant in the garden by summer. Other plants I divided in this way include *Lobelia cardinalis*, pulmonaria and sedum. All of these are excellent plants for dividing and a great way of making your money go further.

8 Dry-shade gardening

When it comes to dry-shade areas, I only plant in autumn and winter. This enables the roots to dig down well into the soil before summer arrives. In an attempt to stop it drying out, we usually put a layer of manure each winter on the South Border, which is a double border. As an experiment 2 years ago, we only manured one side. The difference was incredible. The side without the manure completely dried out and the plants fared badly. However, the manured side came on brilliantly and a quick check below the manure revealed moist soil below.

An obvious, but sometimes forgotten, point is to remember not to put manure or mulch onto dry soil, as you are only sealing in the dryness and locking out the moisture. A layer of about 2–3 inches (50–75 millimetres) of mulch is required and we usually top this up again in autumn and spring just to be on the safe side.

9 Box hedging

One of the most common mistakes made with box is planting it too deeply. The top one-eighth of the root ball should be above the existing soil level.

We clip the box hedges twice a year with mechanical cutters. This is done in mid-May and mid-July, but before August, as late growth gets frosted.

10 Miscanthus

When asked, as I frequently am, to recommend plants, I wouldn't hesitate to say miscanthus. They can be huge, but this is not a good reason to fear them. Remember, they are far better behaved than most unruly bamboos. I began collecting miscanthus 4 years ago and haven't stopped since. We have over forty different miscanthus at Airfield.

11 Propagating euphorbias

I owe a debt of gratitude to my mother for many things, not least of which is the gift of life. More importantly, in my eyes, she introduced me to the wonders of collecting euphorbias. She began collecting them a few years ago and she has since passed on her addiction to me. I now have a collection of fifty different euphorbias.

With over 2,000 species, euphorbia is one of the largest genera of flowering plants and allows for very diverse collections.

Taking cuttings from euphorbias can be a little difficult, but is essential to do so for named varieties. Take cuttings between April and June. Take tip cuttings from the new base growth of about 10 centimetres long. From a health-and-safety point of view, wear gloves when taking cuttings, as euphorbias contain a milky white sap that is toxic. Brian, who used to work with me in the garden, rubbed his eyes with sappy hands while taking cuttings. Once the sap comes into contact with the eyes, it is extremely painful and can cause temporary blindness, which Brian learned the hard way. To prevent the sap leaking from the cutting, you can plunge the cuttings into nearby garden soil, powdered charcoal, sand or hot water for 2 minutes. This clogs up the stem and is sufficient to stop excessive loss of sap. I often just bring my pot of cutting compost to the plant and stick the cutting into it, covering it with a plastic bag straightaway. Someone even suggested putting your cigarette ash onto the end of the cutting, but, since I have been off cigarettes for 3 years, I use the other methods. Make sure that the cutting never dries out. Some heat will help it along, with lots of light, though not direct sunlight.

12 *Sedum* 'Herbstfreude' and its tendency to fall over

This plant was originally called *Sedum spectabile* 'Autumn Joy' but is now known as *Sedum* 'Herbstfreude'. The problem with the plant is that it often flops over. Falling over is caused by excessive feeding or moisture. I dig up my plants every 3 years and ruffle the roots before planting them a bit deeper. They should last without falling over for a further 3–5 years.

Much to my annoyance, I noticed when I was digging them up that the roots were covered in vine weevil. Chemicals have to be called in for this most stubborn of pests. We spray with Armilodox or Pravado. Unfortunately, sedums are devils for vine weevil; a pity, since I was beginning to collect them in the last year and they are one of the best plants to attract bees and butterflies.

Melianthus major **and how I grow it**

Melianthus major is one of the most beautiful plants for foliage and, when crushed, the leaves smell of peanut butter. Its hardiness depends on getting it well established before it gets attacked by a severe winter like the one we had in 2000–2001. I have good specimen clumps in the South Border in Airfield and I recently planted ten more in the new borders in the Walled Garden. Our top growth usually survives the winter and is then cut back to the ground in April. Cutting it back will produce a compact mass of foliage.

One year I didn't cut it back and just let it continue to grow throughout the summer to allow it to flower. The reason for this was that I had seen it flowering in South Africa, its native habitat, and the flowers were amazing, way beyond comparison with anything we have seen here. However, what I ended up with was a gangly plant with eight ugly, spiky flowers about 8 inches in the air. Remember, melianthus hates wind but loves sun and well-drained soil. Plant it with *Verbena bonariensis* and purple cannas for a great effect. This is a good plant for sheltered coastal areas.

The secret to growing *Verbena bonariensis*

Some plants, while not especially striking or flamboyant, are incredibly useful when it comes to creating a picture in a bed. *Verbena bonariensis* is one such plant. This stemmy plant is 5 feet (1.5 metres) tall with very few leaves.

It is not very attractive on its own but I like to plant it under other plants so that it grows through them. It has sumptuous purple flowers and is perfect for attracting bees. A friend of mine, Anne Walsh, told me that the secret of over-wintering this plant is to lift it from the soil in the autumn and plant it in pots. Keep the pots in a polytunnel or glasshouse through the winter and replant in late spring. Pinch out the first few shoots in spring to encourage branching.

I have sown *Verbena bonariensis* many times and it has not survived. However, outside my apartment it seeded into the cobble lock and grew without any soil, nor water, and with the staff walking over it. You never can tell.

It is one of those plants that goes with absolutely every other plant. I saw it growing with *Patrinia* scabiosifolia and the combination was truly stunning. Trial and error never fails.

15 Visiting other people's gardens

Remember to visit other people's gardens as often as you can. In Ireland, we are spoiled for choice and there are gardens to suit all tastes. The garden staff at Airfield try to go on a few garden outings a year and it has to be my favourite way to spend a day off. It is great to see how other people garden and, if you do see an idea you like, don't be afraid to copy it. In September 2001, Sean (one of my team from Airfield) and myself visited gardens in Wales. You need a car for this kind of trip, and don't waste space with suitcases, because, believe me, you will need as much space as possible for plants.

If I had to pick a few particular gardens, I would certainly include Altamont in County Carlow as one of my favourites, especially with the stunning new borders. The walled garden at Malahide Castle in Dublin is worth a visit, as is Woodstock in Kilkenny for its trees, Belvedere at Mullingar for the parklands, Sandylane in Enniscorthy for its large collection of unusual plants, and, for more tender plants, Kilravock, County Cork. Creagh Garden also in County Cork is one of the most romantic on the island, while Mount Stewart in County Down has some of the best designs, planting and all-round atmosphere to be found.

Assumpta Broomfield

Ballyfin, County Laois

Assumpta Broomfield trained at the National Botanic Gardens in Dublin. She has worked at the Dillon Garden, Birr Castle demesne and at Altamont, County Carlow, where, with Robert Miller, she designed and planted the Corona North commemorative border. She has just completed a herbaceous border at Knockabbey Gardens, County Louth, where she is plant adviser. She has a nursery at Ballyfin – Irish Country Garden Plants – which specialises in herbaceous and rare plants.

Assumpta's tips

The easiest way to have a beautiful garden is to get the essentials right at the beginning, not after 20 or 50 years of struggle. So, what are the essentials?

1 Weeds

Certain weeds – like bindweed, bishop's weed and scutch-grass – are like malign dictators. They are determined to be in total control and use every method possible to dominate. There is no way of negotiating a compromise. Before planting, spray with Roundup, wait for any survivors to recover, then spray again and, if they persist, spray again. Do not, under any circumstances, start planting until perennial weeds are eradicated. After planting, do not allow any annual weeds to reach the flowering stage.

2 Soil

Soil varies considerably in different parts of Ireland but, within gardens, generally falls into two categories – good and bad. It's good if it has sufficient nutrients for plants to grow well, is pliable enough for the roots to travel and if there is enough of it. If you're not sure what is topsoil and what is subsoil, look at the ground when a digger is working in your area. You will notice that the top layer is darker – this is the topsoil. The next layer is the subsoil and it is usually lighter in colour. To grow plants well, a layer of topsoil at least 12–15 inches (30–40 centimetres) deep is needed.

If your garden is a mix of subsoil, topsoil and builders' rubble, then make the most important gardening decision you will ever make and remove it. Order a skip, get a mini-digger or wheelbarrow and get rid of what cannot be put right. It may seem an enormous task, but it's amazing what can be done in 1–2 days. When choosing new topsoil, bring in a gardening friend to advise you.

3 Nutrition

The amount of nutrition needed depends on the plants you choose. For a herbaceous border, plants are grown close together and are expected to perform continuously from May to October. This means that a regular supply of food is required over a long period. Ideally, before any planting, the ground should be double-dug and a layer of well-rotted farmyard manure incorporated.

Begin at one side of the bed and dig out a trench 12–15 inches (30–40 centimetres) deep. Remove the soil and retain for the last trench. Spread a layer of farmyard manure in the bottom of the trench, then dig a row of soil adjacent to that trench and put this on top of the well-rotted manure. Work along the bed in this way and cover the manure in the last trench with the retained soil from the first row. Not only does the farmyard manure give nutrition, it helps retain moisture, if the soil is free-draining, and earthworms, who adore it, help to aerate the soil. It is a balanced diet that helps plants to grow and flower well. If farmyard manure is not available, then dig in compost.

4 Compost

Compost is rotted vegetation. This includes leaves, vegetables (uncooked) and all the material from cutting back herbaceous plants and grass. When making a compost heap, separate the weeds from the rest of the material. There is no point in creating problems in the future by helping to spread weed seeds and roots. Some weeds can be composted safely, but, until you know which can and which can't, get rid of them all. Put them in a bag, tie a knot, and say goodbye.

There are a few simple rules for successful composting. The more finely chopped the material, the quicker it will rot. Allow air in at the sides. Cover the top to keep the rain out. If you have the space, have two bays; when one is full, turn it over into the second. This allows air through and also means you have access to the most rotted part. This compost may be acidic, so, if you are growing plants which really like lime, then sprinkle some lime on the compost as it is being made.

5 Free-draining soil

If the soil is too free-draining and the plants wilt after a few days of sunshine, then add farmyard manure, compost or peat to it. Cover the soil with a mulch. A mulch is a layer of material which is spread between the plants on the exposed surface of the soil. It can be spent hops, bark, coir or spent barley grains. I prefer spent barley grains. It looks good, prevents the soil from drying out in summer and adds nutrition.

6 Waterlogged soil

If the ground is water-logged the whole year round, then grow water-loving plants. If, however, it dries out in summer, then take drastic action. There aren't too many plants which like to sit in water all winter and dry out in summer. Put in a drain.

Decide where you can let the water drain to – where is the lowest point? – and put in an outlet. Alternatively, build a soak hole. This is simply a deep hole filled with stones which the water drains into. Soak holes are built all over the country to take the sink-water off houses and they work very successfully.

7 Planning the garden

Think, think and think again. Stand in the garden and note which views should be retained (the Sugar Loaf) and which eliminated (a neighbour's washing line – which has no great aesthetic appeal, unless your neighbour is Vivienne Westwood). Stand in the kitchen or living room and note which areas can be seen from the house. Consider how windy the garden is. Does it need protection? Where is the wind coming from? You may need to plant a shelter belt and allow it to grow before you start planting the garden.

A peculiar shape or uneven land is not necessarily a disadvantage. Great order can be brought to an awkward-shaped garden by having a symmetrically shaped area within it. Equally, uneven terrain gives scope for many possibilities, so don't get in a digger and level the whole area.

8 Choosing trees and shrubs

When choosing trees, always consider their eventual height and spread. There is nothing as ugly as a butchered tree, so don't plant a tree that you will later have to maim. Also, consider the size and density of the leaves, whether the tree bears flowers and berries and whether the bark is attractive.

When choosing shrubs, don't just consider their flowers but also bear in mind how they look for the rest of the year. Do they become ungainly and need pruning? When and how should they be pruned?

Do not plant too closely together. Over-planting of trees and shrubs results in none of them growing properly.

Choosing herbaceous plants

Beauty is in the eye of the beholder, but, that said, some gardeners have good taste and some don't. The cleverest gardeners are able to see how a plant, insignificant in itself, can complement and enhance those around it. Consider where the plant is going to be planted, its height, the size, shape and colour of the flowers, the size, shape and colour of the leaves and the time and length of flowering. And, of course, consider whether it should be planted in sun or shade.

10 Maintenance of herbaceous borders

Use bamboos, hazel sticks and garden hoops to support herbaceous plants. Many plants are worth the bother, especially galega and delphiniums. With delphiniums, cut back some of the emerging stems in spring. This enables the remaining stems to grow even stronger and also ensures a second flush of flowers later.

Dead-head – i.e. remove – old flowers. This will mean that the plant's energy will go into producing new flowers and is vitally important for galega, *Campanula persicifolia* and *Campanula lactiflora* and, of course, for sweet peas.

11 Propagation of herbaceous plants

There are a few herbaceous plants that don't like to be disturbed, but, in general, herbaceous plants need dividing every 2–3 years. If a plant has a single central stem, then it cannot be divided, otherwise it can. Plants vary, so treat each plant differently. The new growth is at the outside of the plant, so, when dividing, always include some of the centre and some of the outside in each division. Some plants naturally separate when gently tugged apart, otherwise use a bread knife or saw to divide the roots. Replant, spaced so that, as the plants grow and spread, they look like a large clump rather than a number of individual plants.

12 Propagation from cuttings

For successful cuttings taken in summer from the current year's growth, spray with water as soon as they are cut, insert into a mixture of peat and sand, cover with plastic and place in a warm but shaded position. For grey-leaved and hairy cuttings, do not cover with plastic but use horticultural fleece or muslin instead. When they have rooted, remove the plastic or fleece and leave for 2–3 weeks before potting up. The cutting material should be taken from the growing tips of plants.

Conifers, vines and evergreens are grown from hardwood cuttings taken in September and October. These root the following spring.

13 Propagation from seed

I always test large seeds by placing in a glass of water. If they sink, they're usually fertile. If they float, they usually are not. Seeds should be collected when ripe on a warm evening. Dry as one would air clothes and then store in a cool, dry place. Sow seeds as soon as possible, usually immediately if they originate in a cold country, or the following spring if they come from a warm climate. Of course, if seeds come in a packet, follow the instructions. Root development is best if some rough sand is mixed with the compost.

14 Pests and diseases

It is best to spray roses before the leaf buds open. This prevents diseases starting in the first place and, most years, this is the only spraying I do. Also, if slug pellets are put down in February, they are most effective. Vine weevil is the most vicious pest that attacks plants. The young grubs are white with a brown head and eat plant roots. The adults are dull grey with a pointed snout and eat leaves, leaving a notch at the edge of the leaf like the notch on a train ticket. If a plant doesn't look healthy, examine the leaves. If they are aphid-free and do not have slug bites – more rounded than those of the vine weevil – dig up the plant. If there are grubs at the roots, kill them. Also destroy any grubs in the surrounding soil. Primulas, saxifrages and heucheras are particularly prone to vine weevil, so avoid growing these unless you are prepared to dig them up twice a year to clean them.

15 Autumn cleanup

Begin the autumn cleanup in late August and cut back herbaceous plants which have finished flowering. This enables the plant to develop new growth and to look good throughout the autumn. In late September and October, cut back all herbaceous plants that are not in flower and remove the waste to the compost heap. To discourage slugs, remove any fallen leaves. Divide and replant herbaceous plants, especially those which have flowered throughout the summer. Feed with farmyard manure or garden compost. This cleanup is essential to enable light in to spring-flowering plants.

Finally – around Christmas – remove old leaves from hellebores and spray with Citricidal (available from health shops) to prevent fungal infection.

Rosemary Brown

Bray, County Wicklow

I was brought up in Enniskerry. My parents were both keen gardeners. My mother was very knowledgeable and had many gardening friends. I helped her and learned as I was growing up. I had my first garden when I was 5 years old. It was about 6 feet (2 metres) square and had an old damson tree, a 'Caroline Testout' rose and madly clashing annuals.

I became an art student at the Metropolitan School of Art in Dublin, in Munich and London too, and my interests were travelling abroad and painting. During the 1939–45 war, I joined the FANY (First Aid Nursing Yeoman) and drove ambulances. I had several gardens at that time – a window box in Belfast and a sandy, windswept patch in Wales. In the 1940s, my parents moved to Old Conna Hill, now Aravon School, the home of my great-grandfather, Phineas Riall. There I learned more about formal planting and rare shrubs.

John and I had our first garden on a roof in Kensington, London. It was a collection of old ammunition boxes placed amongst the chimneys, and in them we grew runner beans, pelargoniums and annuals. Later we moved to Berkshire, where we had a cottage garden of roses, shrubs and perennials, a plum tree and hens. I was secretary of our local flower show and once invited the flower-arranging expert Constance Spry to judge our flower arrangements (and she came).

We moved to Graigueconna (in Bray) in 1970. The house belonged to the Riall family from the 1840s. Phineas Riall's grandson, Lewis Meredith, laid out the garden, which included a large rock garden. He ran a railway line down the centre of the garden and pushed trucks of rocks to the bottom to construct the alpine garden. Many of the original trees and shrubs remain, but we spent many years replanting the borders and woodland.

We grow tender plants, roses and clematis and avoid using chemicals (especially insecticides), thus encouraging wildlife, including a fertile gamecock.

Rosemary's tips

1. Place a square of garden fleece under pots of seedlings to deter slugs and snails. This should be larger than the area of the pots.

2. Chicken food containing bran, etc., placed on saucers under cover (preferably a piece of slate but a begonia leaf will do) will attract snails. Beer in yoghurt pots under cover attracts slugs. Inspection should be carried out each morning and molluscs removed.

3. Keep a bantam or gamebird. They are superb eaters of vine weevils and small slugs, etc. Cocks do less damage to the garden than hens – but keep an eye out for foxes.

4. If you stop using insecticides, the wild birds will eat the aphids and hedgehogs the molluscs.

5. Clean out ponds early in the year to avoid damaging frogspawn. Frogs eat snails.

6. Plastic water bottles with the bottom quarter removed make excellent mini greenhouses for cuttings and seeds in small pots. The lid can be unscrewed for ventilation once the cuttings have struck or the seed has germinated.

7. If you are using wire to stake a shrub, always thread it through a piece of strong plastic hosepipe.

8. Green or plastic netting placed over freshly sown grass seed will deter birds.

9 Lilies and large bulbs planted in plastic pots will fill gaps in the border. Black pots will be less noticeable than red ones.

10 Painting the handles of garden tools red makes them easier to find.

11 Always tie a large coloured tag onto the tool-shed keys.

12 Never put off visiting a garden, especially when you are overseas. The opportunity will probably never occur again.

13 See as many different gardens as possible. You can get ideas for your own.

14 It is easy to carry trowels, secateurs and other small garden tools around in a bucket.

15 When planning a job at the far end of the garden, never look to the right or left on your way there – otherwise you will never reach your destination.

Brian Cross

Lakemount, Glanmire, County Cork

How quickly time passes. I remember, at the age of nine, smelling the scent of Sweet William grown from seed and giving it to my grandmother at Easter. As luck was on my side, I inherited a site ideal for gardening. Originally a chicken and fruit farm, it had rich acid soil and was south-facing, overlooking the River Lee. My interest in gardening was nurtured initially by my mother, who gardened enthusiastically until late in her life.

Boundary shelter planting was my first line of defence against the west winds that decimated the garden during the hurricane of the 1970s. Thankfully, it took with it all the Macrocarpa and Leylandii, which have now been replaced with mixed hardy trees and shrubs.

Having trained as an art teacher, my garden has a strong design base: carefully chosen stone textures – cobbles, paving, gravel – complement a vast array of plants. The Gulf Stream enables many tender plants to flourish, particularly those from Australia and South Africa.

For me, the kitchen garden is essential. Here I grow my luxuries – sea kale and asparagus – in company with root crops. Mixed fruits include raspberries and gooseberries, but not currants, as the birds enjoy them too much. Grapes, peaches, pears and plums are autumn delights. A tip: I grow too much for consumption, so I can let the birds have their fill!

After 40 years, my love for gardening has increased. I resent having to work! I am hoping, at 49 years of age, that the best is yet ahead. The *Magnolia campbellii* and davidii, both incredibly slow to flower, are now mature specimens.

The garden is my playpen, an Aladdin's cave of endless pleasures. Yes, even in winter, when I can spot a design error and enjoy it!

Brian's tips

1 In a new garden, first add lots of organic compost with good-quality acid topsoil.

2 Avoid bark mulch, as it locks in the nitrogen. Each year, apply farmyard manure or home-made compost over all the beds.

3 I am a firm believer in overplanting, but do be sure to thin out in time. The bonus is mature plants to enlarge the borders.

4 To frame a view from the house, use fastigiate trees.

5 When planting a boundary, use mixed species that will filter the wind and blend into the landscape. *Rhododendron* 'Cunningham's White', on acid soil, will attain 4 metres in height and the dark green foliage is a perfect foil for birches. I use laurel cut as a hedge on a stone ditch; left unclipped, it creates a tall windbreak in the arboretum.

6 Always have a kitchen garden, however small. Fruit trees – apple, pear, plums and cherries – can be grown in cordons. I underplant with herbs and French beans.

7 Use sheep wire (a galvanised wire mesh), which is easily moulded to the required shape, to support alstroemerias, aconitums and poppies.

8 When building a greenhouse, have a 'lean-to' and use the wall for a peach. I planted a vine, moved from my great-grandparents' garden 35 years ago, and now what a pleasure it is to eat the fruits on cold September mornings. A narrow path with soil beds is essential for growing tomatoes, cucumbers and peppers.

9 When designing a garden, make the planting complementary to the style of the house. Always cover concrete paths with natural paving material or gravel. Where possible, have beds against the house walls, allowing a 40-centimetre gravel strip between wall and bed to avoid dampness.

10 The dreaded word 'features' may conjure up a picture of white-painted, naked figures. Ponds or summerhouses can make or break a design. Well-chosen objects, when placed in hidden corners, create a visual surprise. If installing a sundial, do not place it directly on the lawn, but lay paving to complement it and check that it is in scale with its surroundings.

11 The only plants I grow in containers are those that tolerate drought through the summer. A good soil- or manure-based compost will retain moisture. Agaves surrounded with bidens can be replaced by clipped box pyramids surrounded by dwarf daffodils and forget-me-nots.

12 I have been using gravel to provide a large part of the textural interest in the garden. Stepping stones through a gravel path encourage one to wander. A new area, my 'river of gravel', leads through a planting of dieramas, grasses, bergenias and irises to the lawn. I never use a membrane beneath the gravel; a 6-centimetre mulch lasts for years.

13 Don't become a plant snob. Drifts of wild primroses under mature trees in spring are a delight. Bluebells in woodland are magical, but, when they seed through the garden, alarm bells should ring.

14 I have waged a war on weeds for 40 years. I am still vigilant. By hand-weeding, you get to know your soil conditions and you may spot a chance seedling, perhaps a new variety.

John Cushnie

Killyleagh, County Down

Gardening is my hobby and my work. I am a garden designer and landscape contractor, working throughout Europe, and a regular panellist on BBC Radio 4's *Gardeners' Question Time* and Radio Ulster's *Gardeners' Corner*. I lecture in Europe and contribute to magazines, national newspapers and websites. My books include *Ground Cover* and *How to Garden*.

I garden on 2 acres in County Down, Northern Ireland. There are cottage areas, water features, woodland, herbaceous and secret areas. A further 6 acres are gradually being converted into an arboretum of my favourite plants.

I hate vegetables and have grass rather than a lawn.

John's tips

1 Don't buy plants on impulse. Decide what to plant in a suitable gap and go and purchase that plant or one with a similar habit of growth. If you only have space for one, then only buy one.

2 When planning an arch, allow sufficient head height for climbers, such as roses, to grow. The width may need to be sufficient to accommodate a wheelbarrow.

3 Many so-called frost-proof earthenware containers will benefit from being wrapped in bubble wrap or hessian in winter. Moving them to the south or west side of the house will help to protect them as well.

4 Shrubs which have made a lot of summer growth may need to be hardened off for the winter. An early autumn application of a high-potash fertiliser will do the job.

5 Don't remove the dead flowerheads from mophead hydrangeas until late spring. They will offer the new, young shoots some frost protection.

6 Old, straggly heathers may be rejuvenated by adding potting compost or end-of-season growbag compost to the bed. Spread the compost over the top of the plants and wash it in to form a layer which the heather will root into.

7 Never apply bark mulch to dry soil. It will shed water, preventing roots from getting moisture. If necessary, water the bed, then apply the mulch.

8 When buying shrubs, check that they have been container-grown rather than containerised. The former will have a good root system holding the ball of soil. If the plant was recently containerised, the compost may fall off the roots, thus causing a check to the plant.

9 Lily bulbs are prone to rotting in wet weather. If water collects around the scales, they will die off. Plant them on their sides on a layer of sharp sand for drainage.

10 Starlings feeding on the lawn can sometimes be a sign of leather jackets. Water the lawn in the evening and cover it with black polythene. Remove the plastic in the morning and collect the grubs, which will have come to the surface.

11 Fasten an old pair of tights over the end of the glasshouse guttering downpipe to prevent leaves and debris getting into the water butt.

12 When using pellets to poison slugs and snails, remove the bodies every morning. They may not be dead and may make a full recovery to munch your plants another day.

13 If you are not hoping to collect seed, remove flowers as they fade. Energy not needed to produce seed will be used to produce more flowers or extra growth.

14 Where bindweed is a problem among plants, insert 3-foot (1-metre) sticks into the ground beside them. As the weed climbs up, it may be sprayed with glyphosate weedkiller without risk to the nearby plants.

Carmel Duignan

Shankill, County Dublin

I garden on a quarter of an acre of heavy, alkaline soil near the sea in County Dublin. I grow a wide range of plants, from fairly large trees to tiny alpines. I am particularly interested in tender plants and am lucky that the garden is sheltered and is not often subject to frost. Despite the fact that the garden is already over-planted, I can never pass a good plant and find it very difficult to get rid of a bad one! I sow a lot of seed garnered from the many gardening societies to which I belong, I haunt garden centres for plants I don't already have and, as often as the finances allow, I cross the water to visit specialist nurseries and never come home empty-handed. Plants are my passion, my pastime and, luckily for me, my living.

Carmel's tips

1. When taking cuttings, I place one small pot within a larger one and put the compost in the space between the two pots. This means that the cuttings are near the edge of the pot, watering is easy and less compost is used. This method is especially useful with late-summer cuttings that should not be potted up until winter is past. When the cuttings have rooted, I remove the inner pot and fill the space with good-quality compost. The cuttings can grow on through the winter without disturbance.

2. I grow many clematis and roses on metal supports. Clematis, in particular, need to be tied in as they grow. I leave plant ties on the supports, so that I always have one to hand when I see straying vines or branches.

3. Seeing ants climbing up into plants is always a sign that aphids are present. They 'farm' them for the sugary substance they secrete. The ants I can do nothing about, but the aphids I deal with!

4. When I buy perennial plants, I always look for those that have as many shoots as possible. These plants can be divided to produce two or more for the price of one.

5. If your garden is small and you want it to appear to be longer, do not plant brightly coloured plants at the far end. The eye is immediately drawn to bright colours. Better to plant the sizzling reds at the front of the garden and the pastel shades at the end. The same applies to large-leaved plants. They also draw the eye and should be at the front of the garden.

6   I always buy the best-quality gardening tools I can afford. In the case of spades and forks, I like stainless steel, lightweight implements. A heavy implement adds considerably to the workload. I am still seeking a shovel that I can comfortably handle. I think manufacturers assume that only strong men use them! Bright colours are essential for secateurs and trowels, so that they are easily found when discarded in the borders. If they find their way into the compost heap, I just have to wait until they appear again.

7   I believe that even the smallest garden should have a tree, but, if something more manageable is required, what about a pole covered with chicken wire and ivy planted around it. The ivy will grow up the pole and it can be clipped and kept at an acceptable height.

8   I sieve my garden compost and add it to a proprietary multi-purpose compost to make a rich mix for my pot plants.

9   I grow ivy on the walls of my garden. It provides good cover for the birds – even if it is also a haven for snails.

10 I have learned to live with the dreaded vine weevil. The best control I know is to re-pot every spring. Every plant that lives in a pot gets this treatment. Spring is when the weevil grubs are at their most active, and the robin just loves them!

11 Grasses are very popular plants and some of the best are a little tender. When they need division, I always do this in spring. They will not survive the winter if disturbed in the autumn.

12 I have only lately started to 'prune up' my trees. This means taking away the lower branches to raise the canopy. The space thus gained can be planted with good woodland plants.

13 Some seeds need stratification before they germinate. This means that they have to be subjected to very cold conditions for a period. I keep such pots of seed near the house and, when frost is forecast, I move them out into the centre of the garden to make sure they get frosted.

14 There is an old maxim that 'you should give a plant away to get it back' and I can testify to the truth of this saying. When I get a new, exciting plant, I try to propagate it. If successful, I give the resulting plant to a gardening friend and hope I won't have to go back and say, 'Do you remember that plant I gave you? Well… I've killed mine!'

15 Finally, a confession of thievery! We are very lucky to have so many good gardens that open their gates to visitors. And I steal from these gardens. No, not cuttings or seeds. Heaven forbid! That is a big sin. I take away ideas – ideas of good design, good planting combinations and good focal points. I don't think the highly talented creators of these wonderful gardens mind too much. After all, imitation is a form of flattery!

Corinne Hewat

Rathmichael Lodge, Shankill, County Dublin

Our garden at Rathmichael Lodge abounds with old-fashioned climbing, rambling and shrub roses. There are numerous borders filled with scent and colour and an all-over feeling of nostalgia and romance. A grass tennis court and a Turkish hazel walk leading to a pavilion add to the air of another age.

Corinne's tips

1. When designing your garden, try to make the style fit in with your house.

2. Be brave with your planting – follow your instincts and try to avoid the fad of the moment. There are an awful lot of hanging baskets, water features and decking around.

3. Stake herbaceous plants early in the growing season. Bamboo canes, chicken wire, branches and metal supports will keep the plants sitting pretty.

4. Bananas are full of magnesium, sulphur, calcium and a load of other goodies. Place some banana skins just under the soil around rose trees and bushes. The roses will love it.

5. Be a dedicated follower of dead-heading. Roses and herbaceous plants benefit greatly from the chop and will continue to flower for a much longer time.

6. Sow seeds when the moon is waxing, not waning, for strong healthy plants.

7. Do not forget to loosen ties on recently planted trees. They need to undo their stays to expand, just like well-corseted ladies.

8. Make manure tea. Steep half a bucket of manure for a day with half a bucket of water. Strain it the next day and then dilute it with more water until it looks like pale amber tea. Soak seeds in this mixture overnight before planting and you are well away. This is the gin and tonic of the garden and will give a lift all round.

9 It is quite possible to plant a rose in a site where a rose has grown already without it getting rose disease (rose sickness). Take away a barrowful of old soil around the plant and replace it with a barrowful of new soil.

10 I find it difficult to sow seeds evenly, but an old farming neighbour of ours, sadly gone, kindly gave me his favourite method. Find a round sweet-tin and bore a hole in the side. This enables the seeds to flow freely but not too quickly. Control at last! Another method is to mix the seeds with a little flour and sprinkle through an icing bag.

11 Cuttings are easier than you think. I have two old fish boxes at the bottom of the garden. I found them on the beach with the bottoms battered and leaking. Perfect! Filled with a mixture of soil and sand (50/50), they provide a perfect place to pop in those cuttings. Roses do well. Take a cutting of about a foot long. Take off the leaves and thorns and leave just a couple of leaves at the top. Leave 4 inches of the cutting above ground.

12 Keep an *Aloe vera* plant on your kitchen windowsill. It is invaluable. Break off a stalk, split it open and rub the juice on your garden grazes, stings, etc. It is very soothing.

13 Visit gardens throughout the year with a notebook, camera and loads of curiosity. Most garden owners are delighted to identify plants – if they can remember the names – and to give you their tips and tell you the source of the plant, shrub or tree.

14 Be generous with your cuttings. Take a few little bags, a trowel and secateurs around with you when showing off your garden to friends. Then, when your precious plant dies, you will have a chance to get it back again.

15 Visit garden centres throughout the year and keep a check on what is new, what is available and what might fit into your scheme of things.

16 Mint is lovely in the garden, but it can become a thug very quickly. Plant it in an old bucket or container and sink this into the soil to within 2 inches (5 centimetres) of its rim.

17 Talk to your plants. Take no nonsense from them. They seem to like it and it improves their behaviour. It has been proved that plants really do like the sound of a voice or music.

18 A garden should not be a show place. It is good to share it, to include humorous touches, to entertain, relax, sit and think in it and to enjoy it.

19 This piece of garden advice was given to me by a dear friend and really is the best advice I know: forget.

Forget

You forget about that unkind thing
that someone said
When you are busy pulling weeds
out of the border bed.
You forget the petty things
that set your nerves on edge
When you're turning up the soil
or clipping at the hedge.
You forget the unfair way
that someone treated you
When you get out in
the garden for an hour or two.
It is strange how quickly
you forget your wants and woes
When you're planting seedlings out
or tying up a rose.
You forget the cares
that make you feel you're growing old
When you see the new green shoots
come pushing through the mould.
Troubles that looked big indoors
will suddenly seem small –
When you're working in the garden,
you forget them all.

Vera Huet

Kilmacanogue, County Wicklow

I've been tricking around with flowers since the year dot, having inherited a love of gardening from my parents, especially my mother. As a child, I earned pocket-money by helping out in the garden and I had a little garden of my own where I grew pansies and snapdragons.

There was no big deal then about colour schemes or Latin names, just plants galore dug in with buckets of manure and flowers remembered more for the friends who gave them than for their names themselves.

Over the years, many different things have influenced my gardening. I love to visit other gardens, discover new plants and share enthusiasms with fellow gardeners. I devour catalogues and books and particularly enjoy the writing of the wonderful plantswoman Marjorie Fish and the sound advice of Christopher Lloyd.

I moved here over 20 years ago to a newly built house surrounded by a wide-open patch of mountainside with a ditch of gorse at the top and bottom. The soil is acid, very stoney and too dry by half! Frost is no problem, but the wind is fierce, checking growth and shredding all before it.

Trying to get a garden established in such an exposed position was painfully slow in the early years. Apart from the fact that I was working alone, a lot of the plants I grew from seed and cuttings; a hungry population of rabbits was an added nuisance.

Now I have my garden over-planted and brimful of treasures, and the greenhouse is chock-a-block with seedlings. Every year I resolve that I will take more care of the plants I've got and add no more. Then my cuttings take root, my seedlings grow stronger, or another catalogue arrives and all my good intentions come to naught.

Vera's tips

1 Hanging baskets

I find hanging baskets hugely useful for everything other than the use for which they were intended:

- I hang them in the garden store, where they are great for holding gloves, string, etc.
- With chains removed and covered in plastic, I have a mini-cloche in the greenhouse.
- I use them to stop my cat reclining on the catmint. The plants can grow through the baskets and the cat can sniff all she likes from a distance without destroying the plants.
- Best of all (with chains removed), I can use them to cover such treasured plants as *Arisaema candidissimum*, *Mertensia virginica* and *Ranunculus aconitifolius* 'Flore Pleno', which are late to sprout in the spring and which can so easily be mistakenly damaged.

2 Labels

It doesn't seem to matter how many packs of plant labels I buy, I still never have enough.

- To mark plants on a short-term basis, I use permanent felt pen on strips of the waxy card of milk cartons and find that they last very successfully for a season or two.
- I find permanent felt pen on chunks of eucalyptus bark works well to label winter-stored dahlia tubers, cannas, etc.
- Plastic labels can be recycled by scrubbing off the old names with a Brillo pad.

3 In a windy garden

I have the good fortune to be surrounded by magnificent mountain scenery that is constantly changing and an absolute joy at any time of year. However, on the debit side, I have to cope with strong winds. Under these conditions, my tips are as follows:

- Avoid aluminium self-assemble greenhouses, as they blow away. Instead, choose a solid hardwood one with strengthened struts.
- When selecting plants, where I find the double- and single-flowered forms equally appealing, I choose *double flowers*. They last much longer. For example, the exquisite little rosettes of *Geranium pratense* last for several weeks, whereas the single form is a waste of space. Ditto with peonies and other plants with fragile petals.
- With the current emphasis on 'feed, feed, feed', my tip for an exposed garden is to go very easy on artificial fertilisers, as the sudden spurt of new growth can be too easily wind-damaged.
- Pinch out the growing tips of plants to get stronger root systems (a must for shrubs). When treated in this way, plants such as verbascums produce very pleasing candelabras of flowers.
- If you want to grow perennials, plan mixed borders so that tall plants like delphiniums can be grown on the sheltered side of shrubs.
- Don't waste money on quick-growing evergreens such as hoheria, *Ceanothus arboreus* and abutilon. They blow down as quickly as they grow up.
- *Photinia* 'Red Robin' makes an excellent wall plant. Its beautiful new growth appears undamaged and there are lovely little white flowers after a sunny summer.
- Ornamental grasses are a great success, adding wonderful movement as they swish and sway in the breeze.

- Old tights are by far the best form of tree and shrub tie, being both soft and incredibly strong. They can be trimmed to disguise their original use (naturally, grey tights for grey shrubs and brown for brown ones!).
- Stock up on green jute twine, as, by the time the 'delphinium wind' strikes and your best staking is put to the test, there will be nothing left in the garden centres except lurid-green plastic stuff!

4 Keep a journal

This is a very worthwhile exercise for jogging the memory. I started keeping a gardening journal about 17 years ago and find it an invaluable record of what plants came from where, and where they are in the garden (a must if you have ten named blue pulmonarias or irises). I love to read back over my notes about gardens I have visited that are no longer in existence, how long it has taken my *Acer griseum* to reach its present height or the first time I heard the cuckoo each year!

5 Make a list

Make a list, especially in springtime when there's so much work to be done. Striking off the jobs that you have accomplished gives a lovely feeling of progress.

6 Greenhouse

My tip is to avoid the 'out of sight, out of mind' trap by keeping a greenfly spray in the greenhouse, so you can give them a quick blast before they get established.

7 Colour schemes

■ I love having flowers in the house and I often find a new colour combination from a randomly cut bunch of flowers that I might not otherwise have thought of – for instance, how lovely apricot colours look with dark blood red.

■ If Vita Sackville-West carried a flower around her garden to see what colours matched it, well then that's fine for me to do too!

8 Fragrance

A bowl of quince scents a whole room beautifully. I find the early fruiting varieties of chaenomeles, such as the dwarf *Chaenomeles alpina*, particularly sweet.

9 Photographs

Take photographs of where your precious bulbs are planted in the garden. I would hate to lose my *Galanthus* 'Hill Poë' snowdrops or my *Narcissus* 'Eystettensis'. Labels get lost and so do bulbs (mustn't overdo the hanging basket tip!).

10 Variegated plants

My tip is to select variegated plants very carefully as regards size, because cutting back and dividing variegated plants often ends up with a lot of shoots reverting to plain green – e.g. *Elaeagnus* 'Limelight', *Lonicera* 'Silver Beauty', etc.

11 Multiplying papyrus

Increase *Cyperus papyrus* by leaving its leaves, arranged like spokes of an umbrella, upside-down in water. Roots will form and these can then be potted up.

12 Playing safe

If space allows, it is well worth having more than one of the same plant in different parts of the garden, especially those of a tender nature. Quite often, after a cold winter, one plant comes through unharmed while the other is killed.

13 Garden for fun

Have a go – be a devil! If there's a loss or two, what odds! There are thousands more plants to try.

14 What not to do

Finally, I've had the same plant in the same soil in the same 3-inch (76-millimetre) pot for 31 years, and it's still alive and well. Can this be a record? What plant could take that punishment, I hear you ask? Answer: *Ceropegia woodii* (poor thing).

15 Time out

Take time out to smell the flowers, preferably at dusk when you can't see any work that needs to be done, and at close range floating on the top of your favourite cocktail.

Angela Jupe

Fancroft Mill House,
Roscrea, County Tipperary

I trained and worked as an architect for almost 25 years and have gardened since the age of four! In 1984, I went to study garden design with John Brookes and set up my own architectural and garden design practice when I returned to Ireland.

Five years ago, I sold up in Dublin and bought an 1840s house and mill in Roscrea, County Tipperary. It had almost no garden, so I have been building a garden over the 4 acres since then. I love building garden buildings, such as my round tower, my glasshouse and, currently, my boathouse on the lake, which I created by diverting the river. I use mainly reclaimed natural materials, such as stone and brick, for these projects.

Plants are a passion for me, especially peonies, old French roses, small-flowered clematis and grasses.

My next project is to start a small garden-design school (in autumn 2002), where people can come to learn about materials and plants and how to use them to best effect. They will also learn how to cook with them!

Angela's tips

1. When designing a new garden, always design from the house out. If the house is two-storeyed, stand at an upstairs window, look down on the garden and imagine it furnished, as you would a room, with trees (tall furniture) to make focal points or to mask a nasty view, strongly structured/coloured flowerbeds (sofas and chairs), a good neutral background of walls or hedges (wallpaper) and large open expanses of lawn area or paving (carpet) to make the garden seem bigger.

2. Aim to have a slightly different view from the window in each of the main living areas and also from the stair window.

3. If the garden space is very contained – i.e. has strong walls or fences surrounding it – create a vista within it to be seen from a patio or conservatory door.

4. Don't have too many bitty features, such as lots of small flowerbeds. One longer, dramatic flowerbed is more effective.

5. If the house is in the country, with good scenic views, don't close these out by having high hedging all round the property. If a high shelter hedge is needed, plant one, but cut a window/door into it to give the best view of the countryside beyond. If you want to keep the wind out, use a gate or mock window with a sheet of perspex behind it.

6   Change levels, if possible, in the garden. Even the slightest change of level, such as creating a shallow sunken grass or paved area, can add a third dimension to the garden.

7   If the garden rises away from the house, consider creating raised, level terraces rather than a sloping garden, with a focal point near the end to keep the eye in the garden.

8   Plant trees to mask out nasty views, such as electricity poles or a neighbouring shed, but find the line of sight from the most used room in the house before locating your tree.

9   Using a small group of trees can be more effective in a small garden than planting only one tree. If the garden is large, a specimen tree, such as a copper beech, a red oak, a walnut or a red horse chestnut, could be used. All of these have wide spreading branches and will eventually mask any unsightly view.

10   Choose hard landscape materials to tone with those used for the house rather than to create a stark contrast. However, don't use too much of the same material, especially if it is made up of small parts, such as bricks. Use large slabs and edge them with a brick border or a central brick infill.

11   Finish your paving with a staggered edge rather than a straight line running parallel to the house, unless, of course, you want a formal look.

12 If the garden is very small, forget a grass lawn. Consider paving it and leaving openings in the paving for plants. Alternatively, gravel the entire area and plant directly into the gravel. The latter is wonderful in a sunny garden, as Mediterranean plants, such as rock roses, sedums and cistuses, will love the heat above and the moist root run.

13 Always leave a sunny area (either in the centre or in a corner) free of planting to sit in and enjoy that glass of summer wine!

14 Plant for height as well as at ground level. If the garden has only low walls or fences, use trellis to raise the wall height or put in metal or timber obelisks and grow climbers such as roses, honeysuckles and clematis over them. The garden will acquire instant scale and height.

15 If using garden ornaments, use one large piece in a small space rather than several small pieces. Sometimes an extra large piece gives great dramatic impact to a tiny area.

16 Group pots of similar materials, but of differing heights, and fill them with exuberant planting. If there are several pots in a group, consider using foliage-only plants in one or two of them to provide a contrast to the flower-filled containers.

Daphne Levinge Shackleton

Lakeview, Mullagh, County Cavan

Daphne grew up with a keen gardening mother, surrounded by the wild flowers of the Shannon callows and the limestone grassland of Lough Ree, near Athlone, County Westmeath. She thinks her first spoken word was 'scutch', which her mother fought endlessly.

A botany graduate of Trinity College, she was popular with the landladies of flats and houses that she lived in, because she always grew vegetables and flowers. She became a real gardener when she married Jonathan Shackleton. She eventually took over the management of the Shackleton garden at Beech Park, Clonsilla, County Dublin, on the death in 1988 of her father-in-law David – a famous plantsman and the creator of the garden at Beech Park. This wonderful garden was then regularly open to the public and was a real source of inspiration to Daphne and, indeed, to many other people.

In 1996, Daphne created a new garden at Lakeview, Mullagh, in the drumlins of County Cavan, bringing with her the spirit and style (and many perennials) of Beech Park. The garden and the surrounding farmland are run to certified organic standards. Increasingly bothered by intensive manicuring and use of chemicals, her style is natural, plant-dominated, relaxed and not quite out-of-control.

Daphne's tips

1 **Some tips for moving a garden**

How often has one heard 'I'll be really sorry to leave my garden'. Well, there's great joy to be had in starting afresh in a new garden and you'd be surprised what plants you can move if you are determined:

- Plan well ahead and, ideally, move your plants in the autumn.
- Create a weed-free holding area rather than keeping plants in pots, which will need attention.
- Line out your cleaned plants in rows. Do not do as I once did, and plant similar species together – such as oriental poppies, kniphofias or crocosmias – as they will grow into each other and become unidentifiable and inseparable.
- *Label* all your plants.
- Watch your plants increase while you get your new garden ready.

2 Organic gardens do not have to look sad and dreary. I use no chemicals in my garden, apart from those occasionally brought in with new containerised plants. Neither do I use cut-off plastic lemonade bottles, old carpets, yoghurt pots or smelly, fly-infested pools of beer. I couldn't live with the ugliness of it. The secret to organic gardening is the recycling of organic waste, with compost as the end product, intensive weeding in spring and early summer and the acceptance of some imperfections and some natural depredation.

3 Think 'compartment' when planning your garden and use colour to achieve a different atmosphere or effect in each area. Choose your colour and stick to it. Separate each area or compartment of the garden with calming sensory-cleaning green planting.

4 Every picture needs a frame and so, too, does every garden. Define the edges of your garden or compartment with a hedge or a structure or through your choice of planting. This is easier in a town garden, but it is important, too, in a garden in the country.

5 Light loads

Joe Lynch, who moved mountains of rubbish, rocks, gravel and soil when he made the garden here at Lakeview, is a wise and wiry Cavanman. 'Little and often' is his philosophy when behind a wheelbarrow. A three-quarters-filled barrow moves at twice the speed of a cumbersome, overloaded back-breaking one.

6 Considerations when laying out a border or flowerbed:

- First decide on and lay out key plants throughout the area to be planted.
- Be more concerned with the shape and size of the spaces between the plants rather than the plants you have put in position. Forget about them, for the moment, once they're positioned.
- These spaces, to be filled later, should allow for an adequate number of groups of plants without them being cramped. Do not leave just a little bit of leftover space that is good for nothing.
- Plant in uneven numbers, in threes, fives or sevens, if possible.
- Don't be too regimented. Break the rules sometimes and put some tall-ish, see-through plants towards the front.

- Nobody gets it right the first time and most plants can be moved easily within the first year.
- Relax and see what happens, and let the plants relax too.

7 These are my top five perennials which no garden should be without, because of their long-flowering period and ease of management:
- Hellebores.
- *Geranium* 'Ann Folkard'.
- *Oenothera odorata* 'Sulphurea'.
- *Aster* x *frikartii* 'Mönch'.
- *Verbena bonariensis.*

8 My top five books that I would never be without:
- The unbeatable and comprehensive *Hillier's Manual of Trees and Shrubs* is a must.
- *Sander's Encyclopaedia of Gardening*, first published in 1895, never lets me down when I need information or am suffering from indecision.
- *The RHS Plantfinder* helps in getting the plant names right and gives an indication of the rarity of your latest plant find.
- Garden visiting is the best way to learn about plants and garden design. Other gardeners' successes and mistakes will give you endless encouragement. *The Good Gardeners' Guide* will help you to discover the best gardens to visit.
- Trailing a bit as it needs updating, but still on my bedside table, is *Perennial Plants* by Graham Stuart Thomas, for its opinionated descriptions of most perennial plants.

9   Use half-hardy annuals generously to infill gaps in the border when early perennials go over. Salvias, verbenas, argyranthemums and felicias are sturdier and flower longer than many true annuals. Cuttings taken in early September and over-wintered, free from frost, should be planted out after the last frosts and will flower continuously and indefinitely in a mild climate.

10 **Make your own hoops for supporting plants in the border**

The best supports for plants are metal hoops of various lengths pushed into the ground at a moment's notice or on hearing a windy weather forecast. We have always made our own, from builders' reinforcing rods cut to suitable and varying lengths, then shaped to a curve by wrapping around a tree trunk and, finally, bending the 'legs' at right angles. Some people then paint them green, but I don't think that this is necessary, as they are not meant to be seen.

11 **Dead-head perennials throughout the summer**

Dead-heading throughout the flowering season is as important as weeding in keeping the perennial border fresh and vibrant. I always compare it to getting a haircut – a small task which dramatically improves the overall effect. Cut a leafless flowering stem right back to the base, otherwise you will have to do it again as the foliage dies down. Many other leafy perennials may be enticed to flower again and again.

12 **Bright, breezy days are for hoeing**

Keeping on top of weeds early in the season, before they seed, saves on weeding all through the year. I absolutely depend on a double-edged (and sharpenable) hoe with a good long handle for reaching between clumps of perennials. A few minutes spent hoeing on a sunny, windy day can mean instant death to weeds in vegetable areas, borders and shrubberies. There is no bending and no need to remove the weeds; they'll shrivel on the spot and return organic matter to the soil.

13 Invest in a sturdy flame-weeder with a double burner

Keeping paths and paved areas weed-free without resorting to chemicals is easy with a flame-weeder. Purchase a big one, fuelled by a gas cylinder, on a pullable trolley. Be prepared to go over the same ground a few times in the season. Keep well away from box, holly and other waxy-leaved plants and bear in mind that plants with lots of dead leaves can go up in flames too.

14 Plant a perennial geranium or a viburnum

There is a perennial geranium for every difficult spot. If in doubt, plant *Geranium* 'Wargrave Pink'. Similarly, there is always a viburnum for every adverse location: try *Viburnum tinus* 'Eve Price'.

15 If you have the space, erect a plastic tunnel

Every gardener should have a plastic tunnel for early vegetables, for propagating plants, for winter pottering or as a 'getaway'. It has revolutionised my gardening life. A minimum practical width for a single-span tunnel is 18 feet (5.5 metres), to give a satisfactory height and to allow comfort when working at the edge of the plastic.

16 Start early vegetables in a tunnel or greenhouse

Get a real head start on the spring by sowing vegetables under glass, where young vegetable plants can also be more easily protected from slugs and snails. Plant early peas in soil-filled gutters indoors. When they are ready to plant outside, dig a shallow trench, lay the gutter alongside and gently manoeuvre the soil and germinated peas sideways into the trench.

17 Plan for the retirement of your garden

Just as one designs and plans for a new garden, should one make plans to decommission a garden when it all becomes too much or when circumstances change? No one should be forced into having and keeping a garden. But would I put this into practice, I wonder?

Iain and
Frances MacDonald

The Bay Garden, Camolin, Enniscorthy,
County Wexford

Iain and Frances MacDonald met while working in the Royal Botanic Gardens at Kew. Frances had previously trained in the National Botanic Gardens, Glasnevin, while Iain had studied at Edinburgh University. They returned to live in Ireland in 1981 and commenced their successful design and landscaping business. They moved to their present garden – The Bay Garden, Camolin, County Wexford – in 1989 and began the process of developing it. The garden has been open to the public during the summer months for the past 5 years.

While Iain still designs and landscapes private gardens, Frances gives lectures, leads garden tours and is a consultant and contributor to radio programmes on gardening. They have also contributed to RTÉ's *Garden Heaven* series.

Iain and Frances's tips

1   When starting a new garden, remember the three Ps: planning, preparation and patience. Our own garden was a neglected orchard. For the first year, we cleared, decided on levels and sprayed with Roundup to get rid of all perennial weeds. The second year, we sowed the lawn and this was mowed for a season; although more than half the lawn is now mixed borders, we have no perennial weed problem.

2   If you move to a new garden, don't be tempted to keep a plant just because it is there. Be ruthless and dig it out if it doesn't fit into your vision for your garden. We retained a large cherry tree for a couple of years before realising that it was out of scale with the character of our new planting. Once it was removed, we wondered why we had ever kept it in the first place.

3   Don't depend on an existing hedge in a neighbouring garden for shelter or privacy. It may disappear if circumstances change, leaving your own garden exposed. Create your own shelter from the beginning. On exposed parts of our garden, we planted a beech hedge 5 years before we managed to develop those areas.

4   If you have the space for larger shelter belts, plant whips rather than standard or half-standard trees. Whips are 1- or 2-year-old plants, usually about 1 metre high, with a trunk about the thickness of a pencil. The advantages are that they are extremely cheap and don't require staking at all. We planted a mixed shelter belt of birch, oak and pine and, in 6

years, the birch have reached 6 metres, the oak 5 metres and the pine 3 metres. The ground beneath is kept clear of weeds and grass by mulching with grass clippings throughout the summer.

5   Preparing for a climber is like preparing for a new baby: you get everything ready before bringing it home. It needs a well-prepared planting hole, one which will enable the plant to spread over time – a wisteria, for example, can live for hundreds of years. It also needs a system of support to suit the particular plant. For roses, wisteria and vines, we use galvanised wire secured with vine-eyes; we place strands, every 30 centimetres, from ground level to the gutters. For late-flowering clematis, we use sheep wire secured to the wall. There is nothing sadder than seeing a climber that has turned into a bird's nest at the top of the bamboo cane on which it came home.

6   When planting a shrubbery, spacing is everything. To avoid overcrowding and unnecessary pruning in the future, use short-lived plants (such as lavender, hebes, cistus, brooms and herbaceous perennials) to fill gaps between slower-growing permanent shrubs. Over the 10 years since the initial planting of our mixed borders, the shrubs which give them structure still have space to grow, while some earlier, short-lived companions have been consigned to the compost heap. The herbaceous perennials have been lifted, divided and replanted a couple of times to keep the composition intact.

7   Designing your borders is like writing a composition: don't mix your metaphors. For example, woodland and Mediterranean plants

require different growing conditions. They don't grow together in nature and they don't thrive or look good planted together in the garden. Utilise the different microclimates within your own plot. Knowing where a plant originates can help you decide on the area in which it will grow best.

8 We are all advised to plant herbaceous perennials in groups of three, five or seven, in order to create drifts for greater impact. This can prove expensive. Again, patience comes into play! Choose your plant carefully at the garden centre, buying a well-filled pot. This plant can be cut into pieces with an old bread knife, repotted and grown on for a few months before planting out or repeating the process. Most of the areas in our garden take 2–3 years from conception to completion. During this time we multiply our stock plants, thus enabling us to achieve the effect we require at minimal cost.

9 We all impulse buy on occasion. A small nursery bed is essential to avoid reproach from a neglected plant left waiting at the back door. Shrubs or trees can be plunged directly into the bed in their containers and herbaceous plants can be planted temporarily while you are deciding on and preparing their ultimate destination.

10 Although very few people give their lawn the attention it deserves, it is an important part of the garden. A mown lawn with uncut edges always looks shabby and takes away from the garden. Make trimming the edges part of your routine when cutting the grass – use long-handled shears, not a spade. Every 3 years, we sharpen and re-cut lawn edges with a half-moon. In some parts we have used a paved edging to give permanent definition to the layout. This has the advantage of enabling plants to spill over from the beds without killing the grass.

11 Aim for permanent plants in your containers to give a year-round display, boosting it with the odd dash of colour from bulbs in spring and tender perennials in summer. Mix commercial, peat-based compost with equal amounts of sterilised loam for your containers – this prevents the plants from drying out too quickly. A layer of bark mulch over the drainage crocks also helps to retain moisture. Top-dressing with ornamental pebbles stops compost being washed out when watering and also helps to display the plant to greater effect. Some of our most effective permanent plants in containers at our north-facing back door are sarcococca, osmanthus, variegated holly, clipped daphnes and phormiums.

12 From mid-summer on, we collect seed from many of our hardy perennials. Check the plants regularly to watch for ripening seed – a hardy geranium can disperse all of its seed overnight if not collected in time. Harvest seed on a dry day. We store them in old yoghurt pots (labelled) until we have time to clean and packet them for storage. They are sown the following spring. Plants that have proved easy to germinate are most of the hardy geraniums, campanulas, many grasses, knautia, eryngium and salvias.

13 Although it is no longer even mildly acceptable to steal cuttings from other people's gardens, stealing ideas and adapting them is another matter. Very few gardens are truly original. Our *Vitis vinifera*

'Purpurea' was greatly enhanced by planting *Clematis* 'Perle D'Azur' to grow through it – a combination lifted directly from Sissinghurst. We all write down the names of plants we see in other gardens, but it helps to take a note of the surroundings and associated planting.

14 Since we started our garden, we have always made compost from garden and nursery waste. However, our life was changed when we acquired a proper compost bin for our household waste. This was essential, as we were reluctant to put this material into our open compost bay in case we attracted rats. This works very successfully, as long as layers of more bulky garden waste are added occasionally.

15 We do an overhaul of our beds once a year, usually in late winter or early spring, depending on the weather. We make it a rule to start in a different area each year. This means that fresh enthusiasm and thoroughness is brought to bear on a new plant each year and the whole process doesn't become a chore. Remember, we all garden because we love it, so take time to walk about and enjoy the garden.

Catherine MacHale

Rochestown Road, County Cork

Like all sensual pursuits, Catherine insists that gardening is not for the fastidious. The marks of a committed gardener are, she says, 'broken fingernails, scratches and insect bites, and a decent ridge of muck on the boots or wellies'! For all that, her love affair with irises and clematis continues year after year. While the erythroniums, crocuses and snowdrops at Glenmahon herald spring at pianissimo level, the irises in May open in a triumphant crescendo, absolutely self-confident in their splendour, shining like jewels in their perfectly tended setting. Everything at Glenmahon comes to perfection.

Catherine McHale does all her own planting, cutting back, designing, construction work and grass cutting. She may look slight, but she certainly can get things accomplished! She loved this site on the Rochestown Road from the moment she laid eyes on it and she has been toiling with it ever since. Twenty years ago, it may have been a well-tended, run-of-the-mill suburban garden, but today it is a plantswoman's dream.

She may not paint with a trowel or garden with a brush, but her way with shrubs and ornamentals is unique and we can best appreciate her garden by simply standing back and admiring what we see. A modest and rather shy person, Catherine typically sees herself as a custodian of the garden rather than its owner. The garden is lucky to have her.

Catherine's tips

1. An alternative use for hanging baskets is to attach one to the top of a metal pole or rod so that climbing clematis can turn and grow down again.

2. Place an upturned hanging basket on an emerging plant that is in need of protection against traffic – in a gravel area, for instance.

3. Place a collection of corks from wine bottles at the bottom of terracotta pots to add bulk without weight.

4. An alternative kneeler is a piece of good-quality carpet in a strong plastic bag, preferably one with a handle.

5. When weeding, search for weeds – such as bittercress – that have grown directly at the base of plants.

6. A long bamboo cane can be used to lift floppy plants off the grass when mowing round the edges.

7. Strim the edges of the lawn, and then remove the clippings with a leaf vacuum.

8. Garden material will compost more quickly if it is shredded.

9. To prevent the shredder getting clogged, make sure that all material is kept dry.

10. A thin layer of soil, seaweed or manure will speed up the decomposition of material that is being composted.

Lorna MacMahon

Ardcarraig, Oranswell, Bushypark,
County Galway

The garden at Ardcarraig was started in 1971 and now extends over 4.5 acres. Originally, the property consisted of a newly built house on a bulldozed site of 1 acre with no topsoil. Over the years, small purchases of adjoining land were made and these included a hazel wood, a stream, a bog field and a rocky hillside.

The front garden is fairly conventional. It is planted with specimen trees, shrubs, dwarf conifers and heathers. It is linked by a border of ornamental grasses to a sunken Mediterranean garden, patio and large herb section. The back garden consists of a series of twelve com-partments cut out of the hazel wood. These include Japanese-style areas, a moss garden, pools, a bog garden and a natural rock section.

Hostas, Himalayan primulas, meconopsis, rhododendrons, heathers and dwarf conifers predominate, as they thrive in areas of high rainfall. Gardening in the west is a challenge, as there are continuous Atlantic gales, 69–72 inches (175–182 millimetres) of rain and poor soil.

Lorna's tips

Wind

1. Avoid planting evergreens in windy positions in the autumn. Keep containerised evergreens in a sheltered corner and plant out in spring.

2. Stake herbaceous plants early. Use hazel brushwood for supporting plants, such as alstroemerias, perennial lobelias and tall campanulas, while they are still small.

3. Select compact and low-growing varieties of plants if they are being planted in windy areas.

4. Some shrubs that are excellent in exposed areas do not thrive in waterlogged soil (e.g. olearias, *Elaeagnus* x *ebbingei* and hydrangeas).

Frost

5. Avoid putting tender trees or shrubs in key positions, as the gap will be more noticeable if they succumb to frost.

6. Avoid planting frost-tender plants at the base of slopes or in hollows, as these areas are usually frost pockets.

Rain

7. In areas of high rainfall, it is more effective to use organic fertilisers. If using chemical fertilisers, it is better to use slow-release ones, such as Osmocote, as they do not wash through the soil too quickly.

8   In areas of high rainfall, it is important to select plants that tolerate wet conditions. Single roses rot and flop less than double varieties. Semperflorens begonias and impatiens are rain-tolerant bedding plants.

9   Moss thrives in wet areas. It can be effectively checked by treating with four heaped tablespoons of sulphate of iron dissolved in 10 litres of water. This is economical and does not burn the grass.

Predators

10   Some plants can help to prevent attack from other insects and animals. Nasturtiums help prevent aphids, while onions planted among the vegetables help deter rabbits.

11   When collecting slugs and snails, it is effective to drop them into a bucket of water containing washing-up liquid, which kills them immediately.

12   Sprinkle a light scattering of slug pellets around susceptible plants – such as hostas – in January during the first mild spell. This will kill a large number of slugs and snails before they have time to breed.

Herbicides

13   To eradicate convolvulus, unwind the leading shoots and push into a plastic bag (leaving the stems growing in the soil), spray Roundup onto the leaves in the bag and then tie the neck of the bag. Leave for 12 hours, then remove the bag. This avoids the need for 6 hours of dry weather, as is usually recommended.

14 To kill 'mare's tail', use one part of Verdone selective lawn weedkiller to ten parts of water mixed with wallpaper paste. Either paint or wipe the solution onto the weed. A woollen glove worn over a rubber glove speeds up the wiping process.

15 The 8-foot by 16-foot (2.44-metre by 4.88-metre) metal grids that are used to reinforce concrete are excellent for trellises, arches and supports for roses and clematis. They are very economical and long-lasting, but they do rust.

16 For indoor bulbs with flowers that require staking, place used cotton reels in the pots when planting the bulbs. The roots, as they develop, will anchor the reels and barbecue sticks can be inserted in the central holes for support.

Robert Miller

The Walled Garden, Altamont Gardens,
Tullow, County Carlow

After graduating from the National Botanic Gardens, Glasnevin, in April 1998, I started a nursery – Irish Country Garden Plants – with a classmate, Assumpta Broomfield. We specialised in Irish cultivars and unusual and rare plants. We also provided a service of propagating plants for gardens open to the public. These included the Dillon Garden, Belvedere Gardens, Birr Castle and, of course, Altamont Gardens. In 1999, after the death of Corona North, we took over the management of two-thirds of the walled garden at Altamont, where, with the help of a lot of Corona's friends, who provided plant hoops and moral support, we designed, built and planted the Corona North commemorative herbaceous border.

In October 2000, Assumpta and myself decided to dissolve our business partnership and I took over responsibility for the running of the walled garden at Altamont, where I now maintain the Corona North commemorative border and run my business, Altamont Plant Sales.

Robert's tips

1 Weeding

A bucketful in February is a barrowful by March; a trailerful by June, by August is a lost cause.

2 Correcting mistakes

During the summer, when your borders are in full bloom, use your camera to highlight mistakes you have made and then use the photographs in the winter to remind you to rectify them.

3 Division of perennials

When dividing perennials, the spade is often the preferred tool, but I have found that using an old handsaw will give you a more precise and clean cut and also lessens the risk of twisted ankles.

4 Pruning

You will often have heard the tip of pruning your roses to an outfacing bud, but, if you want to create an upfacing plant, do the opposite and prune to an infacing bud. This is also suitable for holly and laurel and many other evergreens.

5 Filling spaces

You will often find that, by late summer, spaces arise in your borders. You can rectify this problem by potting up some plants in large containers earlier in the year and then placing these into bare spaces late in the summer.

6 Dry flowers

July and August is the time for thinking about what dried-flower arrangements you would like to have during the winter. At this time you should be collecting and drying your flowerheads, including alliums, cornflowers, globe thistles and many others.

7 Planting a tree

When planning a new planting, especially a tree, it is a good idea to build a mock-up of the height and spread of the proposed tree. This will give you a good idea of what it will eventually look like and where the tree will cast shade.

8 Protection against slugs

I find that a good covering of freshly fallen pine needles is an effective protection against slugs attacking your vulnerable plants – in particular, hostas.

9 Watering

A bucketful of water at planting is worth five thereafter.

10 Plant support

Sixty euro spent on plant hoops will save you 60 minutes of your time.

11 Dead-heading

Dead-heading is the key to having continuous flowers in a good herbaceous border.

12 Buying garden tools

Save before you spend when buying your garden tools.

13 Plant names

Don't worry too much about plant names. It is better to have a plant without a name than a name without the plant.

14 Plant losses

If you sometimes lose some of the so-called tender plants (penstemons, for example), it may be because you cut them back too early in the year. Wait until late spring.

15 Vine weevil control

Most people tend to get rid of any plants they have that are susceptible to attack by vine weevil. I do the opposite. I hold on to these plants and, in late winter–early spring, I dig them up, go through the roots and remove any vine weevil I find. I have discovered that this lessens the attack on other less susceptible plants. You will have at least one good friend during this process – the robin.

Verney Naylor

Bantry, County Cork

Verney Naylor has gardened since she was a child, but it was geology that she studied at university (Trinity College Dublin). In the 1970s and 1980s, she ran her well-known gardening classes using her own garden as an example. During this time, she wrote about gardening for *The Irish Times*.

From the beginning, Verney was often asked by her pupils to give individual consultations in their own gardens. This inevitably led to designing gardens, which she has been doing now for 25 years. She is a full member of the Garden and Landscape Designers' Association.

Two years ago, she left her beloved Sandymount garden when she and her husband moved to West Cork, where she is currently creating a new and totally different garden.

Verney's tips

1. Are you starting a new garden, or even just a new bed? Then make sure you have got rid of every scrap of perennial weed (scutch grass, bindweed, ground elder, etc.), even if it means delaying planting for a whole growing season. This will save you much anguish in the future.

2. Never allow weeds to seed themselves. A counsel of perfection, I know, but – I promise you – it really does work. You can virtually eliminate weeds from your garden within a few years.

3. If you have time to do only one thing to spruce up the garden before visitors arrive, then neatly cut the edge of the lawn. Nothing else has quite the same immediate impact.

4. Broad beans are easy to grow. When there are six flower trusses, nip out the green tops of the plant and cook and eat them like spinach. Cutting them back like this helps to control blackfly – as does growing summer savory at the roots.

5. Grow alpine strawberries from seed one year and they will continue to seed themselves for ever. They make a pretty edging, are very edible and children love picking them.

6. Never pull a 'weed' if you don't recognise what it is. I have had several uninvited but welcome guests 'arrive' in the garden, such as *Daphne mezereum*. I allow lots of annuals and biannuals to scatter themselves about – you can always pull them up if they put themselves in the wrong places. Suitable

candidates are poppies, foxgloves, love-in-a-mist, hardy cyclamen and parsley. The latter won't grow for me unless I let it grow itself wherever it likes.

7. When you buy a perennial in a pot, see if it can be divided into two or more. In that way, you get several plants for the price of one. Hostas, for instance, take this sort of treatment.

8. The books will tell you to prune *Chaenomeles japonica* (Japanese quince) after flowering in the early spring, but I always do it in the autumn, removing the new growth so that you get to see the flowers, which are on the older wood, more easily. You also get that slightly zigzaggy oriental look to the bare branches.

9. Many shrubs that flower in spring and early summer (forsythia, for example) should be pruned after they have finished flowering, but you can start the process while they still look good by bringing the cut branches into the house for indoor decoration.

10. Never prune a witch hazel or magnolia. You can take occasional twigs for a vase, but, if you do much more than that, the plant is likely to turn up its toes and die.

11. Make sure you create paths that are wide enough for two people to stroll along together – especially between planted borders. Plants should be allowed to flop over onto a path – it looks nice – but you don't want to trip over them. I used to think that 4 feet (1.25 metres) was sufficiently wide, but my new paths will be 6 feet (1.8 metres) wide.

12 If you are planning to colour-theme your garden, remember to follow the idea right through. Do not just consider the flowers, but think also of the foliage, the berries, the bark and the spring bulbs. A rash of yellow daffodils can ruin a purple scheme – white ones would be so much more appropriate.

13 If you are trying to give your garden a revamp, don't do it all at once. There is a danger that you'll – almost literally – get bogged down in the mess. Concentrate on one area at a time and get that up and growing before you tackle the next.

14 Finally, after all the hard work, place plenty of seats around the garden – not just on the patio or terrace. These can be stone, timber or metal, so that they become a permanent part of the design. There's nothing like seats to give a calm, restful feel to a garden, even if you are so busy you never have time to sit down on them yourself!

Anna Nolan

12 Shanganagh Vale, Cabinteely, Dublin 18

My grandmother's garden was always awash with colour and full of flowers, so, from an early age, I was drawn to gardening. However, it took a back seat while I enjoyed my working and gallivanting years, including lots of travel. Love then entered the frame and Sean and I settled into our first house in 1970. There, I focused on a rose garden at the front of the house and got roses out of my system. We moved to our present 1960s-style suburban house in 1977, where the front and back gardens were simply grass and had very poor soil.

I then set out on what has been a hugely enjoyable (also time-consuming and back-breaking) journey to indulge my own creative gardening ideas, which were honed along the way by myriads of gardening books, hundreds of lectures and hours of debate with fellow gardening obsessives.

What do I like? I like the 'bigs' and the 'littles' – tiny trilliums and ones several feet high, major and minor epimediums and silver astelias. Colour is hugely important, not only for its own sake but because it can be used to pull together plants in an attractive association of shapes and forms. I am embarrassed at the number of hellebores I have collected (over 100 at the last count, including many species and doubles). These are underplanted with corydalis, hepatica, snowdrops, leucojum, dwarf narcissi, etc. – all colour-coordinated, of course!

I look forward each year to summer, when there is a change of style – from hellebores, bulbs and woodlanders to perennials, featuring lobelia, monarda, thalictrum, campanula, penstemon and many others.

I am an active member of the Alpine Garden Society and grow many alpines in troughs. Each trough has different soil to suit particular plants and some are placed in the sun and some in the shade to give them the best chance of prospering – and they do.

Where am I after 25 years in this garden? Obviously knackered, but still striving to improve the colour and form of the garden by introducing new plants. Would I like to do it all again? Yes – today's garden is very rewarding and the result of many trials and errors. My plan is that my garden will continue to evolve as long as my pins hold out! My grandmother is my role model – she gardened until she was ninety.

Anna's tips

1 Plan ahead

When first planning your garden, think colour, form and situation (whether it is north, south, east or west-facing). Take your time in deciding your colour scheme. A big, golden garden shrub or tree will look out of place in a pink or purple border (unless you are a Christopher Lloyd disciple).

2 Read up before planting

Before planting any new plant, read up about its requirements, as all plants have different needs. Giving the plant a good start will improve your chances of success.

3 Hellebores

Root out hellebore seedlings growing around the parent plant, as these can take root in the crown of a special plant and, in a short time, take over.

4 Grasses

Grasses look very tatty after the winter. Time spent 'grooming grasses' is well spent. Cut back and rake out all dead and brown bits. Smaller grasses can have dead pieces combed out with an old kitchen fork. When grasses have been groomed, it is time to 'fiddle with ferns'. In late spring, cut off all old fronds to make way for emerging new ones.

5 Leaf-mould

Rake leaves into bundles and run them through the lawn-mower. This should speed up their decomposition into wonderful leaf-mould.

Frogs

A small pond brings wildlife, including frogs, into the garden. Frogs help greatly in keeping the slug population down.

Plant-saucers

Unglazed terracotta plant-saucers should be painted with a silicone paint, which will make them non-porous and stop the water leaking onto your conservatory floor.

 Compost

Use all gardening matter and kitchen waste for your compost. Chopping up garden material with secateurs before you compost it will speed up decomposition.

 Planters

When planting up heavy terracotta planters, fill the bottom with broken polystyrene or bottle corks. These provide good drainage and are much lighter than crocks.

Vine weevil

Cut out circles of tights and put them into the bottom of pots to help keep out vine weevil and worms.

Top-dress beds of primula, sedum, etc., with sharp grit to deter vine weevils.

 Getting rid of convolvulus

Fill a jar with weedkiller and bury it to half its depth in the soil. Put in any long strands of convolvulus and leave them to absorb the weedkiller.

12 Escaping roots

Cut circles of tights and put them into the bottom of pots to stop the roots of tropaeolum, etc., escaping through the bottom of the pot.

13 Wheelbarrows

It may be very obvious, but it can save a lot of time and effort if the wheelbarrow is facing in the direction you actually need to go at the start of the job, rather than at the end, when it will be much heavier.

Cyril O'Brien

Knockabbey Castle, County Louth

Kerry-born Cyril O'Brien was one of the most energetic property developers in Dublin throughout the 1990s. Having had his name in the spotlight with projects such as Zanzibar, The Mercantile, Adams Trinity Hotel and HQ Hall of Fame, he has been conspicuous by his absence on the property scene over the last few years.

In 1998, Cyril bought Knockabbey Castle in County Louth, having seen it in the property section of *The Sunday Tribune*. Originally, Knockabbey was to be just another development project and he planned to turn it into a hotel. While he was waiting for the planning permission to go through, he became more attached to the property and decided that Knockabbey Castle would be made into his home and returned to its former glory. This mammoth task has engaged all Cyril's attention over the last 4 years, keeping him away from the Dublin property scene.

Knockabbey Castle has 30 acres of gardens, which, after several decades of neglect, had become overgrown and many of the trees were dead. Cyril employed planting consultants and garden archaeologists to help him realise the potential of the gardens and to make the layout and planting schemes authentic. Where possible, the original plants and trees have been saved and there has also been extensive new planting, which is now maturing. The dilapidated garden buildings have been restored or, where only foundations remained, have been replaced to the original specifications.

While he was researching the history of the castle and gardens, he became so fascinated by the former residents that he decided to open an exhibition devoted to them in the tower-house section of the castle.

Cyril's tips

1 Slugs

There are several ways to deter these slimy garden pests. An easy and inexpensive way is by putting roughly crushed eggshells around the plant. The shells are rough and the slugs don't like crawling over them. To use up leftovers and help out your plants – place an unused melon near plants to attract the slugs, leave it overnight and dispose of it the next day. Alternatively, place petri dishes of beer around your plants; the slugs will be attracted to the beer. If you don't have petri dishes, the lids of jam jars work just as well.

For a more long-term solution, bury wide-topped milk bottles so that the rims are level with the surrounding soil and fill them with a mixture of beer and brown sugar. You will need to dig these up occasionally and dispose of the contents.

For those of you who live near the sea, spread seaweed on your flowerbeds. Not only do slugs hate it, it also makes a great fertiliser. What better way to cut back on your garden jobs!

2 Greenfly

For an organic way to deal with greenfly, boil rhubarb leaves in water and spray the liquid onto your roses.

3 Marigolds

Plant marigolds around the base of roses to deter pests. This also works for tomatoes and helps keep white butterflies away from cabbages.

4 Fertiliser

If you live in a rural area with access to sheep dung, why not make your own fertiliser? Place the dung in a jute bag and soak it in a barrel of water for a few days, stirring occasionally. Dilute the resulting liquid at a ratio of one part sheep liquid to ten parts water and use it to fertilise your tomatoes. Another fertiliser can be made by boiling nettle leaves and leaving them to steep for 24 hours.

5 Flea beetles

Soak elder leaves in a bucket of water for a week and spray the liquid onto plants. Flea beetles in cabbage jump sharply into the air when approached. Coat one side of a piece of wood (about 15–30 centimetres long) with engine grease. Holding the greased side facing down, pass it along the row of seedlings, about 2–5 centimetres above them, as you spray. The beetles will jump up and stick to the grease.

6 Earwigs

To trap earwigs, place a flowerpot upside-down on a cane near the flowerheads. Fill the pot with dried grass or leaves and the earwigs will crawl into it to avoid daylight. Remove the pot and burn the grass once a week. If earwigs still remain a problem, smear grease on the stems just below the blooms.

7 Wireworms

These pests attack plants with fleshy roots and can be trapped by putting a potato, carrot or piece of cabbage stalk on a stick and burying it near the affected plant. Leave part of the stick above the ground as a marker, so that you can remove and destroy the potato, carrot or cabbage.

8 Root fly

To stop root fly in brassica, put a cube of rhubarb at the bottom of the root. Put small collars of felt around young cabbage plants to prevent cabbage root flies going down the stems to attack the roots.

9 Carrot fly

To prevent carrot fly, soak a string in creosote or Jeyes fluid and run it through the upper growth when it is about 2–3 inches (5–7.5 centimetres) high. Grow onions next to carrots, thereby masking the scent which attracts the carrot fly to the carrot. Scatter lawn mowings between the rows every 2 weeks.

10 Ants

To clear an infestation of red ants, sprinkle the area with whole cloves or oil of cloves. If you have ant activity close to the house, place banana skins around plants and rose bushes outside the house – this will attract their attention and keep them outside. Put down a mixture of equal parts icing sugar and borax on a piece of wood or stone near the ant activity and cover to protect from rain. They love sweet things and will devour the bait. They will carry the poison into the nest. As ants eat their droppings, the entire colony will soon be destroyed.

11 Brickwork

To age new bricks, brush them with milk. To make your new patio fit in better with older garden stone- and brickwork, paint on yoghurt or liquid manure and leave to dry.

12 Nettles and thistles

Cut nettles to the ground as soon as they appear. Under constant persecution, they will eventually give up! Remember this rhyme:

> Thistles cut in May return next day,
> Thistles cut in June come up soon,
> But cut them in July and they are sure to die.

13 Black spot

Dissolve four teaspoons of bread soda in water in a jam jar and add a few drops of Fairy Liquid to help the mixture stick to the leaves. Add to a gallon of water in a watering can and apply to the roses. Repeat approximately every 2 weeks. And to help gain time for relaxing in the garden instead of just working, why not add a dessertspoon of Miracle-Gro and feed your plants at the same time?

14 Vine weevil

To rid pots of vine weevil, remove plants from the pot when they have died and pour boiling water onto the soil.

15 Hover flies

Marigolds (tagetes and calendula) planted near tomatoes or roses greatly reduce the frequency of attack by aphids because they attract hover flies, whose larvae devour greenfly by the thousand. Hover flies are the most valuable predators of pests in the garden.

16 Strawberries

When growing strawberries in traditional barrels, put two stones into the bottom of the barrel, nest a length of drainpipe on top of them, then surround the pipe with small stones as you fill the pot with compost. Water the barrel from the top and fill the pipe.

17 Woolly aphids

Climbing nasturtiums trained up apple trees are claimed to control woolly aphids.

18 Buttercups

The buttercup has a nitrogen poisoning quality and it is best not to let it near the vegetable plot. It can stunt the growth of peas and beans.

19 Honeysuckle

Honeysuckle flowers grow in pairs on opposite sides of the stem and were taken to symbolise two lovers, while the clinging climbing habit of the stems also gave the honeysuckle romantic associations. There was a belief that, if honeysuckle were carried into the home, a marriage would surely take place soon after. When growing honeysuckle, keep a close eye, early on in the season, for attack by aphids, they impair the development of flowers.

20 Cabbage root fly

Squares of carpet underlay around young brassicas will deter cabbage root fly from laying eggs.

21 Home-made cloche

Cut plastic bottles into 4-inch (10-centimetre) rings and put these over plants to prevent slug attacks. You can also use the domed part of the bottle as a miniature cloche, as this will save plants from all ground pests.

22 Miscellaneous

- If you are transplanting a large plant, use a tube or length of hose to deliver water directly to the roots during the delicate period after transfer.

- Spray unwanted perfume or aftershave on fence posts to keep dogs away.

- When plants are starting to look withered, perk them up with some cold tea or half a can of coke!

- When pruning larger shrubs and trees, rub wet clay into the cut – this is nature's Band Aid and works equally as well as any commercial product.

- To keep a small area free of weeds for the season, first clear the area thoroughly, then lay old newspaper over the area and cover with bark.

- To help ripen pears and tomatoes, put the fruit into a brown paper bag and add a few nettle leaves. Close the bag and set aside for a few days.

- When pricking out seedlings, hold them by their leaves, not their stems.

- Beat young trees to encourage them to grow.

Maria Prendeville

North County Dublin

I have always been interested in plants and so I decided to make horticulture my career. I graduated from University College Dublin, in the 1950s, got a job with what was then An Foras Taluntais – now Teagasc – and stayed with them until I retired. My work was in vegetables, but, at home, I started out being interested in perennials, then I added alpines and now I'm adding trees and shrubs. However, on consideration, I think my first and last love has been bulbs.

Today I work with the Royal Horticultural Society of Ireland as its president.

Maria's tips

Vegetables

1. Select a suitable area for growing your vegetables. It should have: full sun, good drainage, no competing roots, shelter from wind and no perennial weeds.

2. Do not sow or plant vegetables too early. March is too early for most parts of this country.

3. Do not sow vegetable seeds too deep. Deep sowing means that the seedling uses up all its energy getting to the surface and it will have none left to grow.

4. Tender crops raised indoors do best if planted out under a fleece covering. However, this should not be left on for too long.

5. Pick peas, beans, tomatoes, courgettes and squash while they are still small, and keep picking, or they will stop cropping.

Weed control

6. It is true, 'one year's seeding means seven years' weeding', so remove all weeds at the seedling stage.

7. Mulching the plot will help to keep down weeds.

8. Time the application of the mulch so that the soil has warmed up but has not dried out.

Trees and shrubs

9. Choose a tree or shrub that fits your garden without having to be cut to size.

10 Water newly planted trees and shrubs during any dry spells for at least 2 years after they have been planted.

11 Prune only if you must. Most trees and shrubs do not have to be pruned.

12 Green shoots on variegated plants should be removed at once while small.

Bulbs

13 Do not tie up the leaves of daffodils. Plant the bulbs in the middle or at the back of the border, where the dying leaves will not be noticeable.

14 Plant more bulbs. They fit into the smallest garden and give colour and interest nearly the whole year round.

General

15 Use only fresh seed and potting compost. Months-old compost many not give good results.

David Robinson

Earlscliffe, Baily, County Dublin

David Robinson obtained his Bachelor's degree in Horticulture form Reading University, his Master's degree from Cornell and his Doctorate from Queen's University Belfast. He was Director of Kinsealy Research Centre, Dublin, from 1964–1988 and Guest Professor at the Humboldt University, Berlin, from 1992–1998. He is Past President of the Horticultural Education Association and Chairman of BASIS in the Republic of Ireland. International awards he has gained include the Veitch Memorial Medal from the Royal Horticultural Society, Honorary Life Membership of the International Society for Horticultural Science and Fellowship and Distinguished Horticulturist Award from the Institute of Horticulture.

The garden at Earlscliffe has been developed since 1969 as a low-maintenance garden, with emphasis on rare and frost-sensitive species. The garden covers about 2.5 hectares and has a good microclimate, being close to the sea and sheltered on the north side by the 180-metre high Hill of Howth. Many species that would be tender in the centre of Ireland and in most parts of Britain have been planted here. These include *Cyathea* and *Dicksonia* tree ferns, bananas, *Protea*, *Banksia* and other subtropical (climate zone 9) species. The garden contains many seldom-seen plants, such as *Juania australis, Cordyline bauerii,* the wine palm *Jubaea chilensis* and the Bunya-bunya pine, *Araucaria bidwillii.*

To reduce labour, woody plants have been favoured and very few herbaceous plants or annuals are grown. Weeds are controlled by herbicides and the soil is disturbed as little as possible. Apart from herbicides and slug pellets, no other pesticides are used. Fertilisers are only used on the grass, vegetable and fruit areas and not on trees and shrubs.

David's tips

1. Weeds are probably the greatest barrier in Ireland to trouble-free pleasurable gardening. Getting on top of the weed problem and preventing weeds from seeding rapidly lowers the weed seed population in the soil. This is a major step towards reducing time spent on routine maintenance chores.

2. Used knowledgeably and judiciously, modern herbicides are the key to effective weed control in medium- to large-sized gardens. Under Ireland's frequently wet soil conditions, they are more effective against most weeds than cultivation or hoeing.

3. Cherish your surface roots. These produce vital growth regulators, such as gibberellins and cytokinins, which promote cell division and cell extension. Hoeing around trees and shrubs damages surface roots and is detrimental to plant growth.

4. Herbicides are much more than just weedkillers. When used properly, they enable roots to exploit the fertile, upper soil layers and so stimulate plant growth. They can be regarded as growth promoting substances as well as weedkillers.

5. Roots grow in all directions, upwards and downwards as well as laterally. If fertilisers need to be applied to trees and shrubs, there is no need to fork these into the soil. Although often recommended, this practice inevitably damages surface feeding roots. It is usually better to let plant roots grow upwards into the surface soil layers and absorb fertiliser in this region.

6 If weeds are well controlled without hoeing and plant roots are able to exploit the surface soil layers, there is usually no need to apply fertilisers to trees and shrubs on reasonably fertile garden soil. Over-fertilisation often delays flowering and produces unbalanced growth, which makes trees and shrubs more susceptible to pest and disease attack. Leaves become larger and softer, and more prone to damage by strong wind, and plants are more liable to blow over. In contrast, plants growing in containers where the root system is restricted need to be fed regularly.

7 Where weeds are well controlled with herbicides and plant roots are no longer being continually damaged by hoeing, roots will spread further from the base of a tree than most people realise. Measured from the trunk, tree roots can easily spread the equivalent of more than three times the height of a tree. This information is useful when siting trees in the garden and carrying out routine maintenance operations in their vicinity.

8 In the garden, trees are much better planted as whips rather than as standard or mature trees. Young plants tend to become established and grow way more strongly than older specimens. The stem of a young tree should be able to develop an appropriate trunk taper. If, without support, a tree will stay erect or will return to the vertical after wind, it is better not to use a stake. Without support, the tree will become stronger and less liable to need staking in the long term. A staked tree is also more liable to injury from ties and stakes. However, in some situations staking is needed to protect trees from mowing equipment, vehicles or vandals.

9   If a tree will not stay erect by itself, a stake or stakes will be necessary. There is a tendency for many gardeners to tie a tree to a stake much higher on the trunk than is necessary. If a single stake is used, the trunk should be tied to the stake about 150 millimetres above the lowest point that will enable the stake to hold the tree in an upright position. Tied at this point the tree will be held upright but, above the tie, the trunk will still be able to flex in the wind. Occasionally a tree supported in this way may snap just above the tie. However this risk is worth taking to ensure that most trees develop properly.

10   Trees that are newly planted and left unstaked need to be examined regularly, especially in the first few months after planting, to ensure that they remain upright. If strong wind causes them to lean away from the wind they should be straightened up as soon as possible. Pulling the stem on the leeward side is often all that is necessary to keep the tree upright until new root growth makes it secure. Alternatively, if roots on the windward soil are inclined to lift as the tree leans over, placing a few large stones (or even a concrete block) over the roots on the windward side, as a temporary measure, can have the same effect. Both these methods still enable the trunk of the tree to move in the wind and develop strongly.

11   If a young, fast-growing tree, such as *Eucalyptus*, blows over in its first few years because it has made more top growth than its roots can support, it is usually futile to put in a strong stake and to pull the tree back into an upright position. Where possible, it is usually best to let the tree lie where it has fallen

and to cut the top hard back to a suitable upright branch. This puts the root system and top growth back into balance once more and, with the tree's naturally vigorous growth, the damaged trunk will hardly be noticed the following season. If the root system is damaged when the tree is young, the tree will always be liable to blow over, even if supported by a stake. In any case, staking eucalyptus is not a good practice, as these trees invariably outgrow their stakes within a few years.

12 Similarly, when an older *Eucalyptus* tree blows over, leaving part of the root system intact in the soil, the best practice is to cut the tree hard back almost to ground level. Most *Eucalyptus* species are well endowed with lignotubers at the base of their trunks. Lignotubers consist of a mass of vegetative buds with substantial food reserves and these enable most species to re-sprout strongly when cut hard back. This survival mechanism has evolved over millions of years to enable such trees to survive fire, drought, grazing or other damage to the main trunk.

13 Different techniques are often required when transplanting evergreen and deciduous plants. Evergreens lose moisture continuously because they carry foliage all months of the year and so need to be moved with a ball of soil attached to the root system.

Many evergreen genera, such as *Rhododendron*, *Camellia* and *Skimmia*, have a relatively compact, fine fibrous root system and can be moved easily by this method during most months of the year if watered well afterwards. In contrast deciduous plants can only be moved safely during the dormant period when they are leafless. Trees, such as birch, apple and plum, have a naturally less fibrous, more fangy root system that stretches far beyond the spread of the branches. If lifted with a ball of soil only a small percentage of the root system will be contained within the ball and most of it will be left behind in the ground when the plant is moved.

Deciduous trees with a trunk diameter of up to 60 millimetres are usually better lifted as bare root plants. If trees were planted at the correct depth in the first instance and well maintained without damage to the surface roots, the main roots will be close to the surface and can usually be seen when the surface soil is loosened slightly and the tree shaken gently. The main roots can then be eased or teased out of the ground by a combination of digging underneath and by gently hand pulling individual main roots, starting at the trunk and working outwards. Using this method, the tree will be lifted with a bare, widely spreading root system.

14 At the new location, the tree should be planted, where possible, with its trunk and branches oriented as at the original site. A shallow hole should be dug for the trunk and roots immediately around the trunk. Shallow channels should be dug to accommodate the long main roots and these should be arranged in the soil as far as possible as they were at the original site.

15 Probably the most common fault in amateur gardening, worldwide, is planting trees and shrubs too deeply. When this occurs, damage may not show up immediately, but can inhibit the growth of trees for many decades. Even covering the original root system of some genera, such as *Quercus* and *Fagus*, by as little as 50 millimetres can inhibit their growth.

Other factors can result in trees settling in their planting hole and ending up with their original roots deeper than intended. For example, soil loosened at the base of the planting pit when it is being prepared will tend to settle gradually over a period of years. In addition, any peat or manure worked into the planting hole will gradually decompose, resulting in further settling of the tree. Most trees and shrubs should be planted shallowly rather than deeply. Where possible, the original ground level in the nursery (the soil line on bare root trunks or the soil surface of a containerised plant) should be about 25 millimetres higher than the finished ground level.

Donal Synnott

National Botanic Gardens, Glasnevin, Dublin

Donal Synnott is a botanist, with a particular interest in mosses and the flora of Ireland, and has been Director of the National Botanic Gardens, Glasnevin, since 1993. He takes a dispassionate interest in gardening but is in constant danger of becoming addicted to it. He and his wife garden intermittently in Castlebellingham, County Louth.

The Glasnevin position has brought him into close contact with the world of gardening and with the non-gardener's reaction to it. Conscious of the need to avoid one-eyed visions of the world, and motivated by close scrutiny of the Clycops episode in James Joyce's *Ulysses*, he makes a determined effort to look at gardening with both eyes. He gets little time to write, but an active interest in single malts sometimes overcomes a natural aversion to making notes.

He gives advice only to people who request it but always suggests that students should read *Zen and the Art of Motorcycle Maintenance* and regularly promotes Professor Edward Clarke's belief that horticulture can be fun.

Donal's tips

Doggerel for the Digger

1 Know your own plants

Ask yourself the question:
Do I know my plants?
Can I name each flower
Without a second glance?

Just try out this little game,
Don't pass a plant that you can't name.
In someone else's garden plot
I'm mostly rooted to the spot.

2 Specialise

Impress friends with your latest passion,
Plants that have gone out of fashion.
Willows, ivies, ferns and grasses,
No showy flowers to please the masses.

Green things seem more difficult to name.
Ferns are ferns? All grasses look the same?
They're just as easy to identify
As roses. Cross my heart and hope to die!

Though your neighbour is content
with fern and grass,
Point out he grows *Dryopteris filix-mas*.
He'll tell his visitors and quote you thus verbatim –
The other fern's *Polystichum aculeatum*.

3 Keep a notebook

You must remember this,
A kiss is just a kiss,
But sighs and Latin names of plants

Do not equate with true romance.
Not everyone is truly able
To remember all that's on the label.
'Write it down' is good advice.
You will remember shoes and rice.

4 Participate

Join the local gardening club,
Spend less daylight in the pub,
Have plants to sell at Sales of Work
(Pity 'work' won't rhyme with 'fork').

Be loyal to the club events
In parish hall, pavilion, tents,
The demonstrations, visits, talks,
Annual shows and garden walks.

Think of the committee members
Who give a lifetime of Septembers,
Late retiring, early rising,
Annual programme organising.

5 Don't grumble

When your bedding plants and seeds
Are overrun by annual weeds,
When too many plots need hoeing,
Lawns are overdue for mowing,
When the hedges should be clipped,
When the flower buds should be nipped,
When the roses should be sprayed,
When potatoes should be clayed,
When the prunings should be shredded
And the border plants dead-headed…
Stop. Relax. Take this advice:
Have a glass of something nice.
Of all the seeds that you can sow,
Big aches from little ochones grow.

Take action

If you want the weeds to stay away,
Spray!

Neighbourly advice

Good fences can good neighbours make.
Keep them good, for goodness sake,
But if your neighbours are from hell,
Sell!

Think big

Boston ivy, Russian vine,
Virginia creeper, plants that twine,
Giant rhubarb and sunflowers,
Kiftsgate rose to smother bowers.

These are just a little bunch
Of plants that really pack a punch,
And when your plot's a tangled mess
Repeat the mantra 'more is less'.

Try avant-garde

The restful lawn has had its day,
Cutting grass is now passé,
Wooden decking, coloured beads
Replace the green, reduce the weeds.

Ignore advice from garden savant
If you want a garden avant,
A space with instant pop appeal,
Walls of glass and stainless steel.

A plant or two, a mild placebo,
Integrates the blue gazebo,
Painting of the props and rigging,
Instead of clipping, mowing, digging.

Forget the plans of Gertrude Jekyll
(Remember 'Jekyll' rhymes with 'treacle'),
No more Lutyens classic stonework,
But metal, plastic, rag-and-bone work.

Have no truck with perfect order,
No subtle schemes or well-planned border,
Make no symmetric pools and fountains,
Shut out views of distant mountains.

Tradition makes it very hard,
To embrace the avant-garde,
That moves us on from plastic fawns,
From garden gnomes and leprechauns.

Gardens that are green and charming,
Gardens avant and alarming,
Gardens practical and plain,
Gardens covered from the rain,
Gardens that are crammed with plants,
Gardens that inspire romance,
Gardens alpine, Zen, Feng Shui.
Vive la différence. *Olé!*

10 Take a leaf from Adam's book

In Eden in the days of old,
Adam gardened – so we're told,
Ate the produce of the land
And whatever was at hand.

With blessings from Almighty God
He didn't have to turn a sod,
Use Simazine or Paraquat
Or prune or hoe or sweat a lot.

No double digging, mulching, weeding,
Turnip snagging or reseeding.
He never had to lift or heave,
He just left it all – to Eve.

11 Don't rest on the fifth day

'Let there be slugs,' he said,
'And snails to feed the thrushes
In the trees and bushes.'

A perfect balance lay ahead
In Nature. God had this belief –
But quite forgot the hosta leaf.

For all you hosta zealots,
Don't forget to use the pellets.

12 Practise zero tolerance

Eleven bad weeds that you should hate,
Not let past the garden gate –
Bittercress and celandine,
Horsetail, dock and dandelion,
Willowherb, couch grass and bindweeds,
All those drive-you-out-of-mind weeds,
Groundsel, bittercress and nettle –
Must never be allowed to settle.
'What are weeds for?' I hear you ask.
Don't question. Spray. But wear a mask.

13 Talk to your plants

Treat your plants like dogs and cats
That pay their rent in mice and rats
And faeces, fleas and shaggy hairs,
Scratch-marked doors, upholstery, chairs.

Treat them like a son or daughter,
Give them shelter, food and water.
Neglected pets can scrounge a living,
Potted plants are less forgiving.

14 Read the signs

As monitors along the Nile
Give warning of the crocodile,
So busy lizzie is the first
House plant to flag from thirst.

Creeping cinquefoil shows with ease
When to water bonsai trees.

Plant the fern that's sensitive,
Early warning it will give
To shelter plants that would be lost
If left outside to face the frost.

Dr Mary Toomey

Blackrock, County Dublin

Dr Mary Toomey was born in Ceylon, now Sri Lanka. She trained as a biologist, botanist, entomologist and soil ecologist. She has worked as a university and technical college lecturer and is the author of a number of books on biology and two books on gardening. A keen and passionate gardener from her early childhood days in that tropical serendipitous island, which boasts a rich flora and fauna, she has devoted a lifetime to gardening in Ireland. She is the founder of the Foxrock and District Garden Club and co-founder of the Castleknock and District Garden Club.

During the past 35 years, Mary gardened in large and small spaces in Dublin, and her present small, walled garden is packed to the brim with small trees, shrubs, choice perennials, numerous clematis and other climbers. She specialises in the genus *Clematis*. It is very much an experimental garden, trying out different species and cultivars of clematis, and trees and shrubs play an important role as living supports for romping clematis.

Mary is an international lecturer and, until recently, was the editor of *The Clematis,* the journal of the British Clematis Society.

Mary's tips (for growing clematis)

Clematis are popular garden plants and the genus includes both climbers and non-climbers, the latter referred to as herbaceous clematis. They are very accommodating plants and can be grown successfully in gardens of any size and shape. The tips given below are based on my own experience of growing them in different ways: up walls, fences, pillars, posts, pergolas, arches and arbours; in association with suitable living supports, such as trees, shrubs, roses and other climbing plants; as container plants; and as ground cover.

1. Never be afraid to experiment with clematis in your garden; simply forget about the myths and mysteries surrounding their cultivation. Be courageous and adventurous with them. The truth is that most clematis, once planted, seldom die. They may disappear for a while, but they are well known for rising like a phoenix from the ashes!

2. Do not expect instant results from clematis. Just remember that most clematis, and the large-flowered cultivars in particular, require three or more growing seasons to settle down after planting, in order to establish an extensive, healthy root system, to push up new shoots from beneath the soil surface and to flower profusely. Patience is the name of the game and the aim should be to build up a strong plant with a number of healthy shoots.

   One year's sleeping,
   One year's creeping,
   One year's leaping.

3   It is easy to fall in love with clematis in full flower. However, do not be in a rush. Consider the site, aspect – remembering that most clematis are moisture lovers and dislike hot or baked situations – availability of space, and even your time, which will be needed to prune, train and tie in the new growths and to make a handsome framework, especially if walls are the main supports.

4   Most clematis will grow away happily in semi-shaded or shaded sites, so make full use of every part of your garden to achieve splendid displays throughout the year.

5   Be clever and stagger the flowering of a favourite plant by growing one or more specimens of it facing different aspects. The one enjoying a westerly aspect, for example, will flower earlier than the one facing north.

6   When buying a plant, always look for strong, healthy basal stems. Strong, two- or three-stemmed, bushy plants on short or medium canes are a better buy than single-stemmed, unbranched tall plants on long supports, even if they are in flower.

7   Do not be tempted to invest in clematis 'liners' (young plants in their first pots). They may be cheap but are not ready for planting in the garden or large containers. If you must, grow them on with care for at least another year or so before giving them a permanent position in the garden.

8 If you are a newcomer to the world of clematis, start with easy clematis from the early-flowering group. Species and cultivars of alpinas, macropetalas and koreanas are strong-growing, extremely floriferous and trouble-free.

9 If you garden on deep clay, try the ring-culture method of clematis cultivation. Prepare a deep and wide hole, breaking up the soil if the clay is solid. Incorporate lots of rubble at the bottom of the hole, some well-rotted manure or compost and then plenty of John Innes Potting Compost No 3. Firm the soil. Knock out the bottom of a large bucket or larger wooden container, invert this over the prepared hole and fill it with more John Innes Potting Compost No 3. Plant the clematis in this compost-filled 'container'. The roots will grow and make their way into the soil below the bottomless 'container'. Autumn is the best time to start this method of cultivation.

10 Clematis can be grown in containers. However, not all clematis are suitable for long-term container culture. For a stunning display of summer-flowering cultivars, plant two or three specimens of one type in one very large container with good depth for a single growing season. Do not mix cultivars that have different pruning requirements, or that flower at different times, in one container. Clematis in containers demand diligent routine care, particularly in terms of watering and feeding.

11 Repotting or removing a large-flowered cultivar with spaghetti-like roots from a narrow-mouthed container – however handsome – is no easy task.

Always choose wide-mouthed and wide-based containers with plenty of drainage holes.

12 Some clematis can be grown successfully in containers for 2, 3 or more years, but be sure to prune the roots and repot for good results. Root pruning of deciduous clematis should be carried out when the plant is dormant, while evergreen clematis should be done during summer. Root pruning involves:

- Pruning back the stems to at least 30 centimetres (12 inches) from soil level.
- Easing the root ball away from the sides and taking it out of the container – an old carving knife and an extra pair of hands makes the task more enjoyable and safe.
- Removing 5 centimetres (2 inches) from the side around the whole root ball and cutting approximately one-third off its bottom before repotting.

Spray the foliage of evergreen clematis with water at regular intervals for a few days after root pruning and repotting.

13 Keep an eye on the snails! Trellises mounted on walls serve as resting places for vast numbers of snails during winter months. Make sure that you gather and destroy them before they awaken and before new shoots of clematis appear. Late January to mid-February is a good time for snail-hunting. Free-standing trellises erected a short distance from the walls are strongly recommended for healthy clematis, as well as for ease of training and pruning.

14 Shoots of newly planted and young clematis, which emerge from below soil level during early spring, can be protected with shields made from large, transparent soft-drink bottles with the top cut away. Remove these protective covers as the shoots make their way upward, but be sure to keep a watchful eye on those vertically mobile and agile snails.

15 Lost your labels? Not sure of pruning requirements? Choose three different colours of plastic-coated wire – for example, white for those which require no pruning (Group 1), yellow for moderate pruning (Group 2) and green for hard pruning (Group 3) – and twist them around each plant or its support. Make sure that you write down the colour code for future reference.

16 How much water does each plant require during the active growing season? The amount of water required usually relates to the amount of rain that has fallen. However, plants growing against walls and in containers should be given at least a gallon of water each day during spring and summer, even if there is adequate rainfall. Passing showers never moisten the compost in pots adequately. Gentle, slow watering with a hose is to be recommended.

17 'Roots in the shade, flowers in the sun'? Plant a low-growing shrub or herbaceous perennial in close proximity to the clematis to provide some shade and prevent excessive loss of moisture. Do not use slabs, bricks, stones – they provide hiding places for hungry snails with rasping tongues.

18 When pairing a clematis with a tree or a shrub or another climbing plant, remember not to plant: (a) a very vigorous clematis through a choice, less vigorous garden shrub, tree, rose or other plant, (b) a compact clematis through a large shrub or tree or (c) an evergreen clematis with a deciduous garden plant that requires regular pruning.

19 Do not grow clematis through a formal hedge that requires regular clipping and maintenance.

20 Clematis can be grown as ground cover. Route the stems horizontally and use 'hairpins' made from lengths of strong wire or coat hangers to hold the stems in place on the ground.

21 Some early-flowering (May–June) large-flowered clematis are prone to a fungal disease called clematis wilt (sudden collapse of stems). There is no cure for this. If a plant is struck down by wilt, remove all aerial growth and incinerate them – do not throw them into your compost heap. As a precaution against further attack, drench the area around the base of the plant with a fungicide. Some clematis learn to grow out of wilt and can then grow into strong healthy plants.

Mary Waldron

Narrow Meadow, Lough Owel, Mullingar,
County Westmeath

Ralph and I garden at 'Narrow Meadow', Lough Owel, Mullingar. The long, narrow field on which we built our house 22 years ago suggested the name. Our front garden, which is about 2 acres, overlooks Lough Owel, a beautiful Midlands lake. At the back, we have 4 acres of woodland running down to a boggy area on the fringe of the Scraw Bog.

The Scraw Bog is a protected area, a floating fen in the process of becoming an acid bog. This is a beautiful place in the Midlands/Lakeland area and it is a real privilege to have lived and gardened here for over 20 years.

Mary's tips

1. First and foremost, try to garden in harmony with the environment. Use as few chemicals as you can. Over-use of nitrogen on the lawn, particularly on heavy soils, seems to kill worms, which are a help with aeration. Nitrogen can also get into groundwater and cause pollution.

2. Slug pellets can harm birds and birds control the slug population by eating them.

3. The choice is yours: do you want a sterile environment or one full of birdsong, frogs croaking, lots of free seedlings of your favourite plants and, OK, a few weeds and some blackspot?

4. Pine needles can be used as an effective weed suppressant on acid-loving plants, such as rhododendrons and camellias. Pine needles are also a good slug deterrent. The needles adhere to the slimy one's body and it doesn't like it one bit.

5. Buy a bigger greenhouse than you think you need.

6. Grow something new from seed every year.

7. Prepare the soil into which you are going to plant. Dig it, weed it and feed it with organic matter. This work repays you with years of carefree gardening.

8. Grow the plants that like your soil and situation. This leads to happy plants and happy gardeners.

9. Plant at least one tree for the future. An oak, a beech, a davidia or maybe a *Magnolia campbellii*.

You won't ever see the first two mature and, in the case of the latter two, you may never see them flower, but, if someone doesn't plant them, no one will ever see them in their full splendour.

10 Plant loads and loads of daffodils and crocuses. You can never have enough.

11 Plan your garden to look good in winter and it will look good all year round.

12 Place cuttings near the parent plant, as they seem to take quicker there.

13 Always, always label cuttings when you take them, seeds when you collect them and seeds when you plant them. I can't tell you how many packets of seed I've had to discard as I had no notion of what they were. (I have even sown unlabelled seed and still not known what they were when they germinated.)

14 In June, cut back tall asters and inulas by half. They will grow again and flower well but will not be as tall, which will make them easier to stake. You can do this with quite a few tall perennials, so experiment. It will make life easier.

15 Don't be obsessed with the 'right time' to do things (e.g. pruning or moving plants). Do it carefully when you feel like doing it, otherwise, in my experience, it doesn't get done at all.

16 Be obsessed with your garden and enjoy it. Do as you please with it. Don't be afraid to make a mistake and pay no attention to style gurus – or me, for that matter.

Edna White

Booterstown, Blackrock, County Dublin

I grew up in a large, rambling garden in Donegal. My parents, notably my mother, were keen gardeners – we had a large, walled kitchen garden and always had masses of fruit and vegetables, including exotics like grapes and peaches. We also had lots of good shrubs and trees and a huge, natural-looking rock garden. I picked up a lot of gardening lore from them.

I went to boarding school in Sligo and then took a degree in Modern Languages at Trinity College Dublin. I married a fellow student the following year and we lived in London for 6 years. We came back in 1951 and, after a year of house-hunting, reluctantly bought a new house with an empty garden. It was to have been a temporary home, but, 50 years later, I am still there.

At first I was shocked by the emptiness of the garden, the low walls and the proximity of the road and neighbours, and I planted almost anything green I could find or could afford. Gradually I built up some sort of screening and raised dozens of plants from cuttings. The garden is inescapably suburban, but my (hopeless) ambition was to make it look rural; it is a bit larger than many suburban gardens.

The soil, I was to discover, is light and limey – easy to work and always thirsty – but, over the years, I have improved it. We lived there happily – with three children – and I have continued to live there since my husband's sudden death in 1980. Soon after his death, *The Irish Times* asked me to try my hand at a weekly gardener's diary. At the time it was a very helpful, therapeutic ploy for me – and no end of good for the garden, too, as I had to work away at it to give me something to write about. I did a lot of garden visiting (and still do) to gardens all over Ireland, made many trips to gardens in Britain, made one visit to gardens in the south of France and I have seen many gardens in Australia on the three occasions when I have visited my daughter there. I have made lots of gardening friends.

I wrote the diary for *The Irish Times* for 7 years and retired before I began to repeat myself too often. Now I continue trying to keep control of my garden – with limited success – and, nearly every day, I find in the garden a pleasant surprise or some little bit of cheer to keep me going.

Edna's tips

1 A shake of talcum powder in my gardening gloves ensures that my fingernails emerge tipped snowy white, rather then black.

2 Here is a quick fix for those opportunist weeds and mosses that love to lodge between paving stones and in awkward crannies: sprinkle them with kitchen salt and follow with a libation of near-boiling water.

3 When I'm pricking out a batch of seedlings in mixed colours, I always pot up a few of the smaller, frailer seedlings. I have the (possibly mistaken) idea that these weaklings may become more refined plants with delicately coloured flowers.

4 I often cover vulnerable seedlings that are newly planted out, or small plants, with flowerpots pushed well down around them. This is to protect them, principally, from slugs and the possible vagaries of the weather. I leave the pot *in situ* for a day or two, and then only at night for a further few days.

5 Many cuttings, notably fuchsias, will root in water if left long enough. Put them in a glass container so that you can see the roots as they emerge. When there are a reasonable number of roots relative to the size of the cutting, pot them up in soft, moist soil – be very gentle, as the roots are brittle.

6 The most stubborn garden problem I have ever come across was the spread of an insidious little weed – variously called *Soleirola, Helxine* or mind-

your-own-business – which careered all over a wide grass path and was keen to invade adjoining flowerbeds. I tried remedies both recommended and unrecommended. The recommended remedy, tar-oil wash (Mortegg), will blacken the weed without killing the grass, but, as each tiny plantlet has its own tiny rootlet, it is inevitable that some fragments escape and go on to spread merrily again.

After about 10 years, I gave up and admitted defeat. I had the top sods skinned off and a black plastic membrane laid down and topped with a few inches of gravel. I now have a weed-free gravel path. I liked the look of the green path much better – but my conscience is greatly eased.

7   I did have success with another weed, the dreaded convolvulus, or bindweed. I first noticed the little tendrils of bindweed waving about above the flowers of a large hydrangea and was shocked to find a large colony of the plant growing vigorously and twirling itself around the hydrangea stems. I waited with commendable patience until I had a few hours of unhurried time before tackling the problem.

I cut off the top tendrils and slowly and laboriously unwound the bindweed stems – trying very hard not to break the stems or damage too many of the green leaves. When I had released about ten strands, each about three-quarters of a metre long, I rolled them gently into a loose ball, which I inserted into a plastic bag. Into the bag I administered a lethal spray of glyphosate weedkiller (Roundup). I closed the bag loosely, to keep it dry, and tucked it under the hydrangea, where it didn't show much. Glyphosate works slowly; the poison travels from the green leaves through the stems to attack the roots, which is why it is important not to break the stems. After a few weeks, I found the plastic bag contained only a sludge of rotting stems and hectic yellow leaves. I left it a while longer and then removed it. There were no survivors.

8   Mulch is 'any appreciable top dressing applied to the soil' and is particularly valuable on my dry soil. I hate the look of the popular bark mulch, with its subliminal message that not much work is going to be done in this area. On the other hand, a mulch of coarse grit is both beneficial and decorative around alpine plants, as it helps to keep the crown of the plants dry and the roots moist.

Established shrubs, including roses, of course, and herbaceous perennials, really need a top-dressing of something nutritious and moisture-holding every 2–3 years. Well-rotted manure is best, followed by garden compost, mushroom compost (not for lime haters), enriched peat or even grass cuttings. However, I draw the line at using black plastic, newspapers or old bits of carpet as 'mulch'! I don't mulch around trees – I reckon that they are big enough to look after themselves – but, where it doesn't look too untidy, I like to let them keep the bounty of their own fallen leaves. Never ever apply mulch to dry soil.

9   Runner beans, because they manufacture their own nitrogen, are willing and able to digest uncomposted material. So, in the busy days of spring, I often dig a trench for the beans in advance and use it as a quick dump for non-hazardous weeds and other soft greenery (forget-me-nots often feature). I chop up this layer at the bottom of the trench with a spade and later fill it up with good enriched soil before I plant out the bean seedlings in late April–May.

10 New potatoes often develop scab in my dry, gritty soil, so, when planting the tubers, I like to shield them with a cushion of something soft – like moist peat or grass cuttings – heaped around them in a trench.

11 I love to buy spring bulbs in autumn, but often when I bring them home I can see no obvious place to plant them, so I may temporise by planting them in pots. In spring, when herbaceous growth has died down and most other bulbs are up, the picture is clearer. I might 'plant' the whole pot – wherever I think it looks best – or I may ease the bulbs out of the pot and into the soil, having first moulded a hole in the soil that exactly fits the pot.

12 In a gardening magazine, I read this tip for a winter tonic for lawns and I appreciate the homely, non-metric measurements. Here is the recipe: Dissolve 3 tablespoons of sulphate of iron in 2 gallons of water and water onto the lawn in January. The grass will immediately look greener and livelier and moss will be discouraged, if not actually killed.

Charlie Wilkins

Cork City Suburbs

Charlie Wilkins gardens in Cork and writes for *The Irish Examiner* on a weekly basis. For 20 years, without missing a single week, he has filled a tabloid page with illustrations and text that, put together, could fill half a dozen books. He has yet, however, to even start contemplating such an undertaking!

Charlie lives on a major arterial ring road and insists that he's a 'back gardener' at heart, finding it infinitely more mysterious than the front and far more rewarding in every respect. 'In the back,' he says, 'you can potter in your workclothes and never worry as to who may see you in your haven of seclusion. There, you can create your secret garden, one full of treasures and loved plants, ones usually associated with antiquity, perhaps, but modified into an urban retreat where a little sylvan hoodwinking really works! You can create illusions in the back that could never be attempted in the front – illusions such as growing clematis or climbing roses on wooden supports so that all you own is not viewed in one overall glance. Long, narrow plots can be divided up using specimen shrubs at staggered intervals to the left and right, and paths can be kept narrow and winding so that pollen and coloured petals will have to be brushed from your clothing once you reach that seating area near the limits of your boundary fence.'

Charlie loves bulbs, fuchsias, scented winter shrubs and grass. 'Bulbs,' he says, 'are the gardener's best friend, for they come with next year's flower already made and tucked away safely inside. All you have to do for success is plant them the right way up!'

On his lecture tours around the country, he portrays (and illustrates with slides) the humorous side of gardening. 'Gardening is fun!' he insists and, with his particular brand of Cork humour, he demonstrates this by filling you with enthusiasm.

He has no doubt that something is engendered in, or imparted to, those who work with the soil. In visiting private gardens, he has had ample opportunity to observe at first hand the serenity found in those who dabble in the soil and the solace they get from it. He has not seen or found this in any other hobby, except perhaps painting. 'In some ways,' he says, 'painting is very similar to gardening: one uses a brush and palette knife, the other a trowel and fork; one builds up a picture on a blank canvas, the other, over time, creates one in the bare earth. Both are about expressing a strong idea, and both make your hands dirty.'

Charlie's tips

1. When dividing herbaceous plants, and large hostas in particular, use an old woodwork saw! Slice through the centre of the crown of the plant to make two halves to begin with, then cut these in turn, and so on, until you have the required number of divisions. Books tell us to use two gardening forks, but who has two? I don't, but I do have a saw! Naturally, some material will be damaged beyond use, but, for ease of division, this method is hard to beat.

2. So you own a daphne called 'Jacqueline Postill' and wish you could have more? No problem. Simply spike around the root of your established daphne and, lo and behold, in under 6 months a rush of suckers will appear all around the base of the plant! When large enough, remove these, complete with root system, and pot into individual containers. Allow a further 6 months, minimum, before putting the new plants into their permanent positions.

3. Suffering from thatch in the lawn but really can't afford to hire that scarifier? Afraid that, even if you can afford it, it will do even greater damage? Forget these machines! Try cutting the lawn with the mower set at its lowest setting. You may have to take more than one 'bite' in order to get it cut at this level, but, in the process, you'll remove nearly all of the moss, thatch and raggy growths. Follow with a good feed, watering copiously if the weather is dry. Oh yes, the lawn will look dreadful for about 3 weeks, but, with feeding and adequate moisture, the end result will be excellent. Best month for doing this is September. Second-best month, April.

4 Do you always blacken the lawn when putting on lawnsand? I used to. Now, I water on the sulphate of iron and get immediate results. Use a small teacupful of the iron to 2 gallons of water (a standard watering can takes 2 gallons). Make sure you dissolve the iron completely and do not increase the mixing rate. Any slight blackening that might occur will be gone in days – along with the moss.

5 Don't be afraid to cut back hard any ornamental ivy on house or garden walls. Do this in spring or early summer. The ivy may look dreadful for a few weeks, but it will quickly put out new growth and this will grow tight against the wall. Established ivy that is not trimmed will extend outwards in time, taking up a considerable amount of valuable space.

6 I can't stress enough the need to add grit (small gravel or chippings) to commercial or home-made compost. I like to use up to 40 per cent grit (by volume) in all my mixtures, for it aids drainage and the plants simply love it. Even when planting in the open ground, I always add a bucket of grit to the backfill material and, for my trouble, I seldom – if ever – lose a plant due to wet. This is a must for all those living in high-rainfall areas.

7 Please dead-head your hellebores when they finish flowering. They produce an immense quantity of seed and this germinates like mustard and cress the following spring. These excess plants, if left *in situ,* are, I believe, partly responsible for the fungal infection that attacks these wonderful spring plants.

8   There's only one product for ridding garden paths, walls, brickwork, corrugated roofs, conservatory roofs, stained pots and mould-coated glass of green algae (or any other colour algae) and that's a product called Chloras. Used by the farming community for cleaning milking parlours and the like, it cleans like new all concrete, glass and timber. It is not caustic, but, being a very strong bleach, I recommend you mind your eyes, your clothes and your footwear.

Apply it undiluted to surfaces that have been pre-wetted with water and brush it in with a soft brush. No hard brushing please, just a gentle spreading. Allow it to remain for up to 15 minutes, then rinse it off using plenty of water. The run-off will not damage plants or grass if flushed with plenty of water. In Munster, the product is sold as Chloras, in Leinster it is known as Sterichlor and in the Dublin area it is sold as Eurochlor.

9   Owners of silver birches, especially the Himalayan form sold as *Betula jacquemontii*, can enhance the tree's white bark by washing during spring with a solution of hot, soapy water to which has been added a squirt of household bleach. Tall specimens can be sprayed with the Chloras mentioned above then hosed down with copious amounts of clean water. See the bark shine!

Contributors

Below is a short biography for each of the contributors to this book. Where garden addresses are mentioned, the gardens are open to the public – though on a limited basis or by appointment only. The gardeners listed in this book vary from the professional to the expert-amateur, each with a unique outlook, approach and speciality.

Shirley Beatty

Knockcree, Glenamuck Road, Carrickmines, Dublin 18

Over the last 40 years, Shirley Beatty has created Knockcree, a beautiful garden in the foothills of the Dublin Mountains. She has managed to create a magical and romantic atmosphere in a place where others would fear to attempt such a task. The gardens are noted for their rhododendrons and azaleas and their all year round interest and colour.

Jimi Blake

Airfield Gardens, Airfield Trust, Kilmacud Road Upper, Dundrum, Dublin 14

Jimi Blake trained in the National Botanic Gardens in Glasnevin. In 1993, he took on the position of head gardener at Airfield and, over the last 10 years, has transformed the gardens at Airfield, then overgrown, to being one of the most visited gardens in County Dublin.

Assumpta Broomfield

Assumpta Broomfield trained at the National Botanic Gardens in Dublin. She has worked at the Dillon Garden, Birr Castle demesne and at Altamont, County Carlow. She has a nursery at Ballyfin, County Laois – Irish Country Garden Plants – which specialises in herbaceous and rare plants. Assumpta specialised in the design and instillation of modern, herbaceous borders, and has created some of Ireland's finest borders.

Rosemary Brown

Graigueconna Gardens, Bray, County Wicklow

Rosemary Brown moved to Graigueconna in 1970, where she has developed and maintained the gardens that were created there by the Riall family in the 1840s. Under her management, the gardens, which feature many roses and clematis, have returned to their former glory. In the 1980s, Rosemary was a regular contributor to the gardening pages of *The Irish Times*.

Brian Cross

Lakemount, Glanmire, County Cork

Brian Cross has earned an international reputation by developing one of Ireland's finest private gardens at Lakemount. He is much in demand as a garden designer and is a highly regarded plantsmen. Brian has spent the last 40 years experimenting with the use of vibrant colours in his own garden with a result that is truly outstanding.

John Cushnie

Cushnie Landscapes, 'Mellyn', Shore Road, Killyleagh, County Down

John Cushnie is a regular panellist on BBC Radio 4's *Gardeners' Question Time* and Radio Ulster's *Gardeners' Corner.* He lectures throughout Europe, and contributes to magazines, national newspapers and websites. His recent book *How To Garden* (Kyle Cathie, 2002) has been an acclaimed success.

Carmel Duignan

Carmel Duignan is a producer on RTÉ's *Garden Heaven* programme and contributes a regular column to the *Garden Heaven* magazine. She is also actively involved in some of the country's leading horticultural societies and gives many lectures and talks around the country.

Corinne Hewat

Rathmichael Lodge, Ballybride Road, Shankhill, County Dublin

At Rathmichael Lodge, Corinne Hewat has created one of Ireland's most romantic gardens. Hers is a flower garden that overflows with an abundance of old-fashioned climbing, rambling and shrub roses.

Vera Huet

Kestrel Lodge, The Long Hill, Kilmacanogue,
County Wicklow

Vera Huet is a talented and passionate gardener. She has an extensive knowledge of plants, perennials in particular, and uses colour to great effect in her planting. She specialises in rare and unusual plants.

Angela Jupe

Fancroft Mill House, Roscrea, County Tipperary

Angel Jupe is one of Ireland's best-known garden designers. She trained and worked as an architect for almost 25 years, and studied with John Brooks, the world-famous garden designer. In recent years, she has created one of Ireland's most beautiful and romantic gardens at Fancroft Mill House, which is open to the public.

Daphne Levinge Shackleton

Lakeview, Mullagh, County Cavan

A botany graduate of Trinity College, Daphne married Jonathan Shackleton and, on the death of her father-in-law, became manager of the Shackleton Garden at Beech Park, Clonsilla, County Dublin. In 1996, Daphne created a new garden at Lakeview, in the drumlins of County Cavan bringing with her the spirit, style and many perennials from Beech Park. The garden and the surrounding farmland are run to certified organic standards.

Iain and Frances MacDonald

The Bay Garden, Camolin, Enniscorthy, County Wexford

Iain and Frances McDonald are both qualified horticulturists and run a design business together. At their County Wexford garden, they have indulged their talents as designers and expert plant enthusiasts. Frances also leads garden tours to some of the world's finest gardens.

Catherine McHale

Catherine McHale is a passionate gardener who loves to travel and visit other people's gardens which inspire her to bring ideas back to her own. Catherine gardens in Cork, does all her own planting, designing and construction work.

Lorna McMahon

Ardcarraig, Oranswell, Bushypark, County Galway

Lorna McMahon gardens in County Galway where, overcoming the many difficulties of gardening in the west of Ireland, she has created a stunning oasis. Starting off with 1 acre in the early 1970s, her garden has developed into a series of gardens, which is now ranked as one of the best in the country.

Robert Miller

The Walled Garden, Altamont Gardens, Tullow,
County Carlow

In 1998, Robert graduated from the National Botanic
Gardens. He took over the responsibility of the running
of the walled garden at Altamont, County Carlow, where
he now maintains the Corona North commemorative
border and runs his business, Altamont Plant Sales. His
current interest is in developing the displays of herbaceous perennials within the walled garden.

Verney Naylor

Dromreagh, Durrus, Bantry, Co. Cork

In the 1970s and 1980s, Verney Naylor ran her well-
known gardening classes in Sandymount County Dublin,
and edited the gardening pages of *The Irish Times*. She is
a full member of the Garden and Landscape Designers'
Association. Two years ago, she and her husband moved
to West Cork, where she is currently creating a new and
totally different garden.

Anna Nolan

Shanganagh, 12 Shanganagh Vale, Cabinteely,
Dublin 18

Anna Nolan has created a remarkable garden full of
hellebores and rare plants, and has developed a reputation for using the best garden plants and perennials with
great style and artistry. Her garden, which is open by

arrangement, is full of rare treasures and her plant collection is noted for its year round interest and colour.

Cyril O'Brien

Knockabbey Castle, County Louth

In recent years, Cyril O'Brien has restored one of Ireland's finest historical gardens at Knockabbey Castle. With care and passion, he has brought back to its former glory one of Ireland's best-kept gardening secrets. His careful attention to detail has put Knockabbey Castle high on the list of must-see gardens in the country.

Maria Prendeville

Maria Prendeville is the current president of the Royal Horticultural Society of Ireland, and is well known as a broadcaster and lecturer. She graduated from UCD in the 1950s, and was then employed by An Foras Taluntais (now Teagasc) and stayed with them until she retired. She worked mainly with vegetables and she is regarded as one of the country's leading horticultural experts.

David Robinson

Earlscliffe, Baron Brae, Ceanchor Road, Baily, County Dublin

Dr David Robinson is regarded as one of the country's most eminent horticulturists. His work in this field has been recognised by many international awards, including, the Gold Veitch Memorial Medal form the Royal

Horticultural Society, Honorary Life Membership of the International Society for Horticultural Science and Fellowship and Distinguished Horticulturist Award from the Institute of Horticulture. His garden is noted for its wide range of tender plants.

Donal Synnott

Donal Synnott has been Director of the National Botanic Gardens in Glasnevin, Dublin, since 1993. During his tenure, he has overseen major renovation work, notably the Curvilinear Ranges and the Palm House, as well as the development of the gardens. He also gardens with his wife in Castlebellingham, County Louth. He believes horticulture can, and should, be fun.

Mary Toomey

Dr Mary Toomey is a graduate of Trinity College Dublin, where she trained as a biologist, botanist, entomologist and soil ecologist. A former university and Technical College lecturer, she has written a number of books on biology, She is a co-founder of Castleknock and District Garden, and is the founder and now president of the Foxrock and District Garden Club. Mary is an international authority on clematis and edited the recently published *Illustrated Encyclopedia of Clematis* (Timber Press, 2001).

Mary Waldron

Mary Waldron is known to many for her work with the Royal Horticulture Society of Ireland – she was its president until March 2002 – and as a garden writer for *The Irish Garden*. Over the last 22 years, she has created a garden on 2 acres in Mullingar. Mary believes in a hands-on approach and enjoys experimenting with new and interesting plants.

Edna White

95 Booterstown Avenue, Blackrock, County Dublin

During the 1980s, Edna White wrote the gardening diary for *The Irish Times* for 7 years. Her column is remembered as inspirational by many gardeners and she is regarded as being one of the country's finest garden writers. Though she is now in her eighties, she still finds gardening a source of surprise, consolation and cheer.

Charlie Wilkins

Charlie Wilkins is one of the country's best-known gardeners. He writes weekly for *The Irish Examiner* and draws his experience from his garden in Cork. He travels nationwide giving lectures and is noted for his humorous and light-hearted style.

Index